Golden

Circle

Secrets

Tina

Thank you for

being here. My

Best of you

Golden
Circle
Secrets

How to Achieve Consistent Sales Success Through Customer Values & Expectations

DALE MIDGLEY AND **BEN MIDGLEY**

WILEY

JOHN WILEY & SONS, INC.

Published by John Wiley & Sons, Inc., Hoboken, New Jersey.
Published simultaneously in Canada.

For general information on our other products and services please contact our
Customer Care Department within the United States at (800) 762-2974, outside the
United States at (317) 572-3993 or fax (317) 572-4002.

Wiley also publishes its books in a variety of electronic formats. Some content that
appears in print may not be available in electronic books. For more information
about Wiley products, visit our web site at www.wiley.com.

Library of Congress Cataloging-in-Publication Data:

Midgley, Dale, 1974–
 Golden circle secrets : how to achieve consistent sales success through
customer values & expectations / Dale Midgley and Ben Midgley.
  p.   cm.
 Includes bibliographical references and index.
 ISBN 0-471-71857-2 (cloth)
  1. Sales management. 2. Success in business 3. Customer relations. 4.
Selling. I. Midgley, Ben, 1969– II. Title.
HF5438.4.M53   2005
658.8′1—dc22
                                                         2004022591

Printed in the United States of America.
10 9 8 7 6 5 4 3 2 1

To Memé and Papa Thierry
whose golden circle of love will never end.

Contents

viii   **Contents**

Preface

What you do not want done to yourself,
do not do unto others.

—Confucius (551–479 B.C.)

Right now you are the president, vice president, treasurer, and the secretary for a company called You, Inc. How are you doing? If you are not doing as well as you would like to, then it is time to check the foundation on which you have built your life and your career.

The foundation of You, Inc. is just the same as the foundation of a house; it is what holds everything up and together. Have you built a foundation that emphasizes values and qualities such as integrity, determination, competency, cooperation, leadership, dependability, loyalty, support, and intelligence?

It is these values and qualities that you look for in your employees, associates, and everyone in your life because their presence means that you can trust what you see as being truthful. You want these qualities in the people you work with and also in the people that you work for.

Without them, the foundation of your career will never truly be solid. Instead of attracting good customers and good people, you may drive them away. But if you focus your life on a set of core values, the relationships you have with your family, friends, associates, and all who you come in contact with will flourish, grow, and be strengthened.

Truthfulness with others and with yourself are essential elements of the foundation on which your success and personality are built. There is no substitute for them and they are the measure on which you will judge yourself when it comes time for you to sit back and ask, "How have I done?"

In business these days, values are popular. So, they are given a great deal of lip service, relegated to corporate vision statements, customer service slogans, image advertising, and other superficial means. They are used to help make a quick sell, a fast buck, and rarely anything else. Too many corporations act under the pretense of *having* these values, when in truth they are used as just another means to an end. The result of this selfishness is the erosion of trust in American business.

Many other challenges inhibit productivity in today's corporations almost as profoundly as the lack of values and poor management; however, they are much less obvious. In business, there are interpersonal lapses of values at all levels that cause dramatic interruptions in the productivity and stability of results. These are the things we have all experienced, such as large egos at the office, turf wars, people left out of the "Old Boys Club," discrimination based on gender, ethnic origin, age, or other superficial factors. There are managers who make decisions based on selfish motives, decisions that benefit them rather than the business and its employees. There are people who have their "public face" and their "nonpublic face" depending on who is watching. There can be cheating, trickery, and deception plain and simple. The result is a system that in many cases ends up favoring those who practice weak values, rather than those who practice strong values. Because these lapses in values are harder to uncover than the more obvious corporate missteps we have seen recently, the average person suffers as a result. In this kind of environment, no one wins—for long.

The smartest business people understand that they need hard-working, loyal, productive employees to succeed in good times and in bad. They also understand that people will only give the extra effort that it takes to make the business successful in the hard times if they are treated well.

In other words, American business leaders need to understand that "good business is good business." If more people did what Confucius suggested, we would not have the widespread corruption or lapses in values that cause so many losses—losses in revenue and, much more importantly, losses in human capital.

If we are smart, we will take all of these hard lessons, view them for what they really are and address them as they really need to be addressed. Each of us every day has the opportunity to affect these situations, to better ourselves, and to be great in our business and personal lives.

We have sought out people in our work and personal lives who put a premium on values. As a result, rather than bitterness and disappointment, we have found life to be a joyful, priceless experience. It is to these values and to all who have the courage to practice them every day, that we dedicate this book.

Our purpose in writing this book is to provide you with the tools you need to build a career that is firmly based on a solid foundation of personal values, quality, and consistent performance. This book is about creating and following a system—the Golden Circle of Business—that will enable you to deliver quality *plus* consistency, which will help to produce a healthy income for yourself and a consistent revenue stream for your organization.

It is the ability to stick to those values and deliver a quality product or superior service time and time again that separates the successful professional from the amateur.

Most books about sales provide the reader with the tools to make a simple sales transaction and little else. We liken these books to houses without rooms, structures that may be appealing on the outside but, in reality, are empty on the inside.

We intend to give you more than that, much more. The *Golden Circle of Business* will help you to build a complete house, one that has been well designed to include all of its rooms, a house that is appointed with fine furnishings inside and out.

In this sense, the Golden Circle of Business will give you security, much as a well-built home does. Our system will not only teach you how to generate revenue, it will help you to acquire the skills required to deliver those results year after year, whether you are a salesperson or president of the company.

We've written this book from many years of experience in the business world. It is our mission to provide you with the formula for excellence, a way for you to become extraordinary—something that many people talk about and hope for, but few ever achieve.

If you do, in fact, master the basics that we discuss, the Golden Circle will provide you with a neverending source of income and, more importantly, a continuing reservoir of personal, family, and professional satisfaction. In other words, a secure and happy future.

We wrote this book from the heart. We hope you enjoy it.

Chapter 1

Why the Golden Circle?

When you are good to others, you are best to yourself.

—Benjamin Franklin (1706–1790)

Welcome, as you enter the Golden Circle of Business, we hope that this book helps you take a new look at the relationships in your career, as well as in your life.

We put the time and energy into writing this book for good reason. Between us, we have 55 years of business experience with companies of various sizes—ranging from less than $1 billion to more than $42 billion in sales. We have experienced first-hand many of the challenges that both salespeople and businesses face and how they are handled.

Some businesses handle problems and obstacles very effectively. More often than not, however, they deal with challenges very ineffectively. That is, they use methods that may be appealing in some respects, but serve to alienate employees and drive customers away over the long term.

Why? We can't say exactly. Perhaps the pace of business is too fast to keep up with. It may be that personal pride and ego interfere with making the best decisions for all involved. The problem may also stem from the fact that some managers don't care enough to take the time to do things the "right way"; that is, the best way for the customer, for the employees, and thus, for the health of the business.

Regardless of the reason, throughout our careers, we have seen many of the same, negative scenarios played out time and time again. The unfortunate result is wasted time, energy, financial resources, and most sadly, human potential.

After 12 years of independently analyzing what we've seen, we have both drawn many of the same conclusions that explain how businesses get into trouble in the first place.

Our solution is the *Golden Circle of Business*—the customer-oriented business system or paradigm that companies can leverage to attract and satisfy customers, energize employees, and keep a consistently healthy top line.

We named this paradigm the Golden Circle of Business because, in its simplest form, we view business as a neverending circle of repeating cycles, or concentric circles (see Figure 1.1). While poor decisions beget more poor decisions, all of which radiate throughout the entire organization, good decisions do the opposite; they beget more good decisions, which also affect the entire business.

If good decisions are creating and directing the movement of these cycles, a business will prosper. In other words, it will be "golden," and it will affect and inspire everyone associated with it in a very positive way. You can be assured that in due time, the goodwill will spread like a gust of warm wind and penetrate the industry involved.

Unlike other popular approaches to business, the core of the Golden Circle of Business is a combination of two things: customer values and a sales system. The same principles that enable and encourage a sales system to achieve consistent success can be applied to all levels of

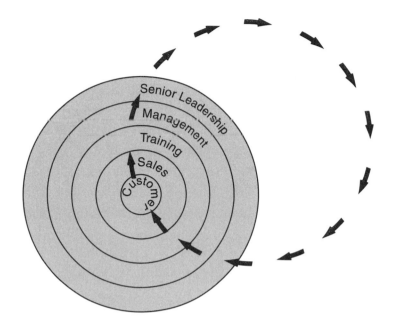

FIGURE 1.1 How the Golden Circle Works

an organization. If these principles are embraced and followed throughout the entire organization, they will create a positive dynamic, and in doing so, will ensure that the business achieves success as a whole.

AT THE CENTER: THE CUSTOMER

The basis for this business system is the customer and what matters most to him or her—more specifically, the customer's values and expectations. Because no business can operate without the customer, there is no more logical place to begin discussion of this business management system.

Our logic is simple: If a company aligns itself with the customer's values and consistently delivers its product or service in accordance with those values, then the customer will consistently utilize the company's offering. Consistent utilization of a company's offering will ensure a healthy top line. A healthy top line, in turn, produces healthy cash flow. Healthy cash flow provides profits and corporate growth, provided the balance of the business is being managed just as diligently and ethically.

Ring One: The Sales Process

The Golden Circle sales process draws its motivations and approach specifically from the customer's values and expectations. Doing so ensures that whenever a customer comes into contact with the business, the customer will be met with and leave with the correct "authentic" experience, a concept we explain in depth later.

When the customer's values and expectations are consistently met or even surpassed, this positive, satisfying experience creates a substantial, sustainable competitive advantage in the marketplace. In addition, customers begin to develop a sense of trust, and soon, your company name becomes synonymous with a high-quality product or service, customer satisfaction, and integrity. Over time, the relationship your company has with its customer base becomes even stronger, which engenders more customer loyalty and goodwill, consistent referrals, and the enhancement of your company brand.

Ring Two: The Training Process

As you might expect, on-going training is essential to providing a consistent, high level of service. For customers to remain satisfied, they must be handled well every time. Training is the key to creating a "belief" in the company's mission and its vision even before its employees have had the chance to experience it personally or put it into practice.

High-quality, on-going training is key for a corporation to maintain a commitment to its employees, a trust with its employees, and to ensure their consistent performance. Training will eventually overlap with and inspire a high-quality customer experience.

The combination of training and experience on a consistent basis fully validates the employee's belief in the company's vision and values. The employee then becomes fully engaged and, thus, lives and sustains the vision and values of the business. Well-trained, committed, satisfied employees inspire increased customer awareness, satisfaction, and retention.

Ring Three: Management Style

A fully committed management team must demonstrate and inspire the following four key values throughout the organization:

- *Mutual respect and dignity* for all employees and customers
- *Intelligence,* both emotional and rational
- *Trust* among supervisors, peers, and subordinates alike
- *Personal responsibility*

For a business to instill these values in employees, the management team must practice them in each and every decision, transaction, and interaction. This must happen at all levels throughout the organization through the daily and long-term management of the business. The positive spillover effect to customers will embellish and enhance the company brand name, giving the company a definite and sustainable competitive advantage over others.

Ring Four: Senior Management Leadership and Accountability

Very often, senior managers find it difficult to keep in touch with what is occurring through all levels of the organization—primarily because they find their schedules full of complex tasks such as strategic planning and financial management. However, keeping in touch is the only way to really know if employees are being properly trained and if the sales and customer service process is truly aligned with customer values and needs. It is, therefore, vital to the success of the business for senior managers to include the following items in their list of top priorities:

- *Creating a process for observing and being involved in the business day to day:* Senior managers must find a way to observe as many levels as possible, and gather feedback on those operations. Without this important process, the information senior managers receive is likely to be filtered through a few trusted associates who may feel the need to please them.
- *Cultivating an atmosphere that allows for expression of candid feedback:* Senior management must insure that management at all levels are willing to listen to feedback as objectively as possible, and see it as valuable information they can use to improve the business.
- *Remain approachable:* Senior managers must be amicable to hearing dramatic differences of opinion. This way, and this way only, will employees feel free to express themselves. This way, and this way only, will executives truly learn the needs of employees and be able to make their top-level decisions based on practical, accurate information from the entire business chain.

- *Creating an infrastructure for continuous free and open communication:* You cannot hope for this to happen or assume it is happening on its own, you have to willfully create a system that will encourage the flow of honest and genuine information—the type of feedback that is the hardest to obtain.
- *Making trust an organizational goal:* To allow for continuing personal growth and accelerated learning, this goal (trust) needs to be measured at all levels and continually acknowledged as vitally important. People learn much more and work much more effectively with, and for, people they trust.
- *Focusing on good management, rather than just good margins:* Good management needs to be the first objective; if it is, good margins will naturally follow.

Above all, senior executives must understand that they are morally and fiscally accountable. But to whom first? One of the greatest challenges set forth by the Golden Circle, is that it calls for senior executives to be accountable to customers first and foremost, then to employees, and then to shareholders.

Most companies operate as if they are accountable to the shareholder first (some even mask that position by saying they are accountable to the employee first) which sets the cycle moving in the wrong direction and inspires short-term thinking. In turn, this points the company in a direction that is likely to be counter to customer values.

The Golden Circle calls for senior-level executives to consistently base their decisions and conduct themselves according to the same customer values that form the basis of the sales process. By doing so themselves, they have a much better chance of ensuring that everyone else in the company is doing so. There must be a common value consensus among all employees, in every level and position in the company, for the customer to receive consistent treatment.

- *Remember that these values start with the sales system and flow upward.* Both the sales process and training system help instill these values throughout the company's entire culture upward, toward the management level, to the senior team. When these shared values guide senior leadership to make decisions that reflect customer values and satisfaction, those values are, once again, reflected downward throughout the company.

Perhaps the best thing about the Golden Circle model is that nothing can be faked; it has to be real. This integrity and interdependence of every level causes a healthy transparency and trust within the organization. Should something go wrong, it will be clear and employees and customers will know. There is a huge advantage to the company that can work this way; the faster problems are uncovered, the faster they can be remedied. Customers hardly expect perfection; what they do respect is openness, honesty, a quick response, and fair treatment. The Golden Circle of Business ensures all four.

Chapter 2

Sales and Your Corporate Culture

There is no business without a customer.

—Peter F. Drucker,
writer, teacher, consultant

Now that you have a general overview of the Golden Circle, before we go much further, we would like to share a story with you.

Cliff Young was an older man who lived on a ranch in Australia and always had a dream to participate in a marathon. So Cliff, after much thinking, finally made the decision to enter a marathon, when he was 61 years old. The one he chose was the Sydney to Melbourne marathon. This is a 500-mile long, multiday marathon, and one of the most grueling in the world. It was said that to finish this grueling test you would have to run for approximately 16 hours a day, sleep for 8 hours, run for 16, sleep for 8, and so on. This was believed to be the only way someone could finish and win the race.

The day came and Cliff went off to Sydney to enter the race. He arrived at the entry station the day before the race was to start to sign up for the marathon. He walked up to the entry table (still wearing his bib overalls and gumboots from the ranch) and told the officials that he wanted to enter the marathon. They took one look at Cliff and immediately pulled out the disclaimer form stating that they were not responsible for any injuries or death. Cliff signed the form and then asked if there was anything he should know about the race. They said no, just be here at 8:00 A.M. in the morning.

Cliff arrived at the starting gate the next day ready to run the marathon. Cliff lined up at the starting line (some even say he was still wearing his gumboots and overalls) and all the other runners looked at him in disbelief, how could a 61-year-old man seriously be running this race? The gun sounded and the race was on. Shortly thereafter, needless to say, Cliff was in last position. The officials looked around at each other and predicted that he would be out of the race before the day was over.

On that first day as the race went on and on for hours, Cliff continued to keep going. He seemed to have everything working against him. Not only did he not dress like the other runners, he did not run the way the other runners ran. Cliff just kind of shuffled his feet and because of that he ran much slower than all of the other competitors. No one even bothered to explain to him the way the race "should be run" if he wanted to have a chance at winning because no one thought it was worth their time. As we mentioned earlier, if you want to win this marathon you are supposed to run 16 hours and sleep 8, otherwise you will never have the stamina to make it. But, Cliff did not do that, he just kept going. He just shuffled along, napped here and there and continued at his own pace. After a few days of this shuffling and brief napping, rather than running 16 hours and sleeping 8, not only did Cliff end up finishing the race, he won the race. And, he didn't just win it, he won it by a day and half and set a record that was in the *Guinness Book of World Records*. Cliff was a national hero and appeared on many TV and radio programs and is a revered icon in Australia.

Because no one thought a 61-year-old man could survive, much less win, this race, the officials never asked Cliff any questions like what do you do for a living? Or, have you ever run a marathon before, and so on. They underestimated him drastically and basically figured he was not worth their time.

As it turns out, Cliff was a potato farmer and he had over a 200-acre section. In addition, he helped his brother herd cattle. So, he spent every day running all around his ranch doing work and herding cattle. Also once he decided to enter, he trained very hard for this race (in his gumboots), so his stamina and work ethic were rock solid. When doctors investigated how he ran, they discovered that his way of running was the best way to complete the race because it did not tax his knees and put little pressure on the leg muscles. Since then, Cliff's record has been broken but only because now, everybody shuffles like Cliff did (Cliff passed away November 2, 2003. He was 81 years old—a legend).

Cliff won the race because he did not follow the "way it has always been done" or the way it was "supposed to be done." Cliff just went out there and did it the best way he knew how, and that is why we are bringing you the Golden Circle of Business.

As a business or an individual, the Golden Circle will show you how to remain on or above target with your sales goals consistently every year. Though some may find it hard to believe, we are telling you that there is no reason any individual or company (which relies on salespeople to move its product or service) should ever miss year after year sales growth targets, it simply never needs to happen.

Now let's look at the evolution of this management process and how it begins with the right sales approach. As we have stated, this book is about making a career, rather than a simple sale. Our paradigm starts with selling for one reason: Selling is fundamental to making things happen in business. In one way or another, we are all salespeople.

If you listen to the financial reports on television, or read any business-related publication, you know that each quarter companies forecast the revenues they expect for that period. In other words, they estimate their sales. How much of their product or service will be utilized because of how much, in one way or another, they sold.

But people don't hand over their money for a product or service easily; businesses first need to attract customers before they can sell them anything. So the first step in building your career is to learn about your customer. Without this vitally important first step, virtually nothing can be achieved.

What things do most customers value? It's safe to say that most of us and our customers look for honesty, integrity, ethical behavior, respect, sincerity, genuine concern, competence, product knowledge, follow-up, and trust.

Although these traits sound commonplace, don't make the mistake of undervaluing their importance.

Without a doubt, they are the essence of every good relationship you will ever have with anyone, including a customer. It is these traits that will draw loyal customers to you for the long term. The challenge is to have the discipline to practice these important values, without fail, in your own sales process on a daily basis. Do so, and you will stand out as exceptional.

If you are a manager, a greater challenge is to do your part in internalizing these values into your company's sales process. As the Golden Circle paradigm exemplifies, to ensure consistency, these values must radiate upward through all the "rings" of your organization.

But where is the most logical and effective place to start capturing these values? The answer is with the sales process. The reason? It's highly likely that the very first interaction a customer will have with your company is with a salesperson. If your sales process fosters trust and customer satisfaction, then strong, enduring relationships will naturally build.

In the Golden Circle, the sales process is the feeder and delivery process that brings customer values into the organization. These values are then enhanced and further applied through insightful training, proper management, committed leadership, and responsible business planning.

This helps ensure that the genuine feeling of trust your customers get from the sales team will be instilled in every facet of the business. Trust is essential; without it, organizational learning and development is hindered beyond measurement. Once instilled, that trust will extend from the employees to the many communities the business serves.

If this can be done, then in any given situation, employees will know with a high degree of certainty "the right thing to do." They will fall back on those values if they are ever in doubt. When employees make the right decision consistently, the whole process builds momentum and is further driven and sustained by predictable actions that are inspired by those same values. As the Golden Circle suggests, these good business practices become circular; there is no end to them.

But how can a sales system really influence an entire business culture and bring in consistently strong numbers? What does it take to build a sales system like this?

Good question. The answer begins with this: The way a company sells reflects everything about the way it does business, including:

- How much it really values and treats its customers
- How it treats, trains, and promotes its employees
- How it fosters employee involvement
- How it views customer service and customer care
- What it values and the ethics it possesses
- How it views innovation and change
- How it views its role in the community

In sum, the way a company sells reveals how much the business respects itself and the customers it serves.

We can say this with a great degree of certainty be-cause it is reflected consistently in almost any company. If you are now or have ever been in sales, then you understand this clearly. If you have never been in sales, you will know this from your own experience with sales-people.

Ask yourself:

- Have you ever worked with a salesperson that did not seem interested at all in you or what you wanted, but only in his or her own agenda?
- Have you found some salespeople to be so rehearsed that they seemed incapable of thinking for themselves?
- Have you ever changed your mind about making a purchase and had the salesperson turn cold, distant, or disinterested? Or, even condescending, pressur-ing, or rude?
- Have you worked with a salesperson who seemed to understand only how much the item in question cost and nothing else?
- Have you worked with a salesperson who described the product or service with so much ambiguity that you were left in a fog with a list of unanswered questions?
- Or, have you worked with a salesperson who seemed willing to explain only as much as needed to make the sale? And, you found yourself with an unwanted surprise once you made the purchase?
- Have you every made an expensive purchase and never heard from the salesperson again?

The way you are treated by a salesperson is almost always a sign of what you can expect from the company. That's because each and every company makes a decision on what sales approach it is going to take with the public. No company allows salespeople to do what they wish; all salespeople have been trained in one way or another. So, if you don't like the way that you where treated by the salesperson, you can be certain that this treatment reflects the way that the salesperson was trained to treat the customer.

But is it worth it for you to complain if you feel that you've been wronged? Will it really matter? The response you will get which you can pretty much predict from the tenor of the initial sales transaction is likely to fall into one of the following four categories:

1. In a "less than average" company, it will go nowhere and do no good.
2. In an "average" company, it will most likely be ignored until you insist on talking to a supervisor. In no way does that guarantee satisfaction. To get some form of acceptable resolution, you'll often have to threaten to contact the Better Business Bureau, an attorney, the media, the state attorney general's office for consumer protection, or another government regulatory agency; all of which requires a lot of time. The average company wagers a customer won't put this time in.

3. A "good" company will listen and acknowledge your concern, but not necessarily act on it. This is because most companies know that upset customers just need to be heard and acknowledged. If the situation *must* be addressed beyond the customer apology and the standard "feel good" protocols, then it will be resolved.
4. A "great" company will take a sales-related complaint very seriously. They will consider it important feedback and do something about it whether or not the customer bought the product or service. The smartest business people will not want to see the same scenario affect other potential customers in the same, negative fashion. They will see the example as a very valuable training tool for their staff and overcompensate the customer for their negative experience. These few, "great" companies understand that the sales process affects so much more than just the transaction itself.

Unfortunately, the majority of companies look at the sales process only as it affects the numbers at the point of sale. They view selling as a one-dimensional function that generates revenue on a daily, weekly, monthly, or quarterly basis. They simply want to make a sale, make it as fast as possible, and take the money and run.

Companies need to view the sales process as one of the paramount determinants of their success or failure and dedicate the appropriate time to making sure it is done exactly the right way. What many companies miss is the exceptional added value that the proper sales approach can bring to the table. What they don't realize is that the proper approach creates three additional lines of revenue, as opposed to just the initial point of sale:

1. Those sales that would be missed with the status quo sales approach.
2. Referrals from the existing sale.
3. Brand enhancement/improved community reputation that drives others to buy the product or service through word of mouth.

A properly conducted sale will always have a compounding effect. All of these revenue streams build over time continuously, thus increasing their impact on the company's success. If not acknowledged, understood, and utilized, these potentially lucrative additional revenue lines will never be developed and will never contribute.

Companies need to look closely at the following issues that are essential to the well-designed sales culture:

- Providing a sales process that the salesperson can continually build on with the client
- Building customer loyalty right from the introduction
- Building customer loyalty without making a sale

- Increasing the chances that the customer will buy the next time, as well as refer others to the company
- Managing the amount and quality of referrals your salespeople receive
- Keeping salespeople producing consistently and feeling good about what they do so you can retain them for a long time

The primary argument for making "more of the sale" and for making the sales process one of the paramount issues a business faces is this reality: No business has a 100 percent closing rate for sales. It's just not possible.

If your sales approach focuses only on getting prospects to buy, if your sales process ends after the sale or when someone walks away without buying, then you are missing out. We view this as the equivalent of giving away half or more of your business's revenue to someone else. Why do that?

Standard sales approaches are also extremely susceptible to economic trends. When the economy is good, the numbers will be good. Likewise, when the economy is bad, the numbers will be bad. How many companies have displayed that pattern over the past few years? In a bad economy, people still buy things. From whom they buy is the point. The right sales approach can help keep a company growing on a consistent basis, insulated from economic downturns and protected from price competition.

If you're a bit skeptical, then consider the fact that consumer spending has really been the only thing that has held off a deep recession in recent years. In the United States, consumer spending accounts for nearly two-thirds of the gross domestic product.

The company with the better sales approach will always win more available sales. If your competitors are primarily price-driven, then creating an "authentic" sales experience is essential to draw customers to your company and for you to stay competitive and achieve your top-line targets during down times.

CONCLUSION

Let's look at 12 questions you need to ask yourself to determine if your sales system is cultivating the three lines of revenue—missed sales, referrals from existing sales, and word-of-mouth sales from your enhanced reputation—that we discussed earlier:

1. Is the sales process really over after the sale has been made?
2. How are customers treated when they choose not to make a purchase?
3. Does your sales approach do anything to encourage those who did not buy to promote your company to others?

4. Do you encourage your salespeople to approach these prospects again?

5. Does your sales approach constantly build your company's reputation with customers and prospects and with others in your community or industry?

6. Do your salespeople know how to build customer loyalty without making a sale?

7. Do your salespeople know how to encourage and stimulate ongoing sales?

8. Do your salespeople know how to sell the company, even if they don't make the sale?

9. Do your salespeople generally feel good about what they do and do they honestly believe in what they sell?

10. Do your customers walk away feeling good that they had the opportunity to work with a salesperson from your company?

11. Does your sales process consistently generate referrals?

12. Do you have consistent producers on your sales team and are you successful in retaining them?

How many times were you able to honestly answer "yes"? You should see even one "no" response as a red flag. It could indicate that you're not selling as much as you potentially could. And, if you are not getting all the benefits from your sales approach that you potentially could, why aren't you?

In sum, the Golden Circle incorporates all 12 of these benefits into its sales approach because it is based on two important goals:

1. Interactions that make a person feel good
2. Interactions that make a person feel valued

It is no secret, really, that these two goals are vital to a successful sales process; any and all of us would respond positively to this kind of treatment. Sadly, only a small percentage of businesses recognize this. If you follow the tenants of the Golden Circle, yours will be among the few that do.

Chapter 3

The Sales Process in Depth

Careful attention to one thing often proves superior to genius and art.

—Marcus Tillius Cicero (106–43 B.C.)

Now, let's look more closely at the Golden Circle selling method. As we have discussed, customer values are positioned at the very core of the Golden Circle. We've built a highly effective sales process around those values and expectations.

The result: Every time a customer meets a salesperson, both the customer and the salesperson feel comfortable because the focus is correct, meaning on the customer. This, in turn, creates trust because the customer feels that the salesperson has the customer's interests at heart. When your customers trust you, they will be much more likely to align themselves with your business, buy your company's products, and refer others to your business.

It's a win-win; you are doing a good thing for your customer, and the customer will, in many cases, want to reciprocate. Because this approach is contrary to the one that most businesses take, it will give the business a distinct advantage in the marketplace, something will just "feel" different about doing business with you or your company.

Now let's look at the status quo: The typical business finds a sales approach that can be taught to the employee easily. The salesperson attempts to sell the product or service to the consumer with the sole purpose of driving revenues. The company assumes that this approach supports the goals of the business.

Generally, these sales systems strive to lead, control, persuade, or outwit people. They may be based on things like price points and the urgency created by time-sensitive promotions. They also tend to be scripted and they broadly stereotype customer tendencies.

The truth is: These systems are "hit or miss," and their results will track the ups and downs of the economic cycle closely because there is no real commonality or connection with the customer. There is no mutual bond of trust. The customer can and most likely will, over time, chose to buy from a dozen companies like this, because there is absolutely no differentiation in the customer's mind.

Businesses using these sales approaches give their employees an all-purpose sales system that is supposed to be used with all prospects, all of the time. It is left to salespeople to make it work if they hope to succeed.

In this case, the only things salespeople really have to work with are:

- Pure determination
- The strength of their own personalities
- Their willingness to "break the system," if necessary, to make a sale

The only other option is to just follow the system, and settle for any results that come their way.

Taking the latter option will at best lead salespeople to some success, a lackluster closing rate, of perhaps 30 percent to 50 percent. The reason? The nature of any sales system is inherently limited if its goal is to "close the deal." This is where most companies miss the boat. While it is true that every company has to "hit the numbers," most don't even recognize the importance or the value of addressing basic human needs and desires when it comes to sales. It has just never really been a requirement in the world of selling.

Human nature cannot be controlled or ignored; rather, it must be respected and worked with. Today's consumer is diverse, which is why a standard step-by-step sales approach or technique that is applied to all prospects doesn't work consistently. Let us give you a few reasons why:

- Have you ever seen a house that had some ridiculous lawn ornament in the front yard?
- Have you ever asked yourself, "How could he or she wear that?"
- Do you know anyone who let's their dog sleep on the bed?
- Do you know any couples that just seem to argue all the time?
- Have you ever read a bumper sticker that says, "If you do not like my driving dial 1-800-eat-_ _ _ _?

- Have you ever met anyone who just seems to think that they are a little bit better than everyone else?
- Have you ever known someone who has lost a loved one and has never really been the same since?
- Have you ever seen someone do or say something that just made you think to yourself, what where they thinking"?
- Have you ever known someone with cancer?
- Have you ever known someone who inspired you?
- Have you ever met anyone who seemed to be able to laugh anything of?

Some of those things may ring a bell, some may not, but the point is there are many people out there with different views of life. To waste any time trying to fit all those views in to the same sales system is nearly pointless.

For consistent sales, salespeople must align themselves with customers (something we review in depth shortly), and use a well-rounded approach to selling; one that increases the customer's desire to buy and heightens the chance that the sale will be made. What salespeople need most is the authentic experience that the Golden Circle sales process creates for the customer.

Think about what an authentic experience means to your customer and what it does for a business. By definition, it is unique to your business. Because it cannot be duplicated, it makes your business stand out, regardless of the number of competitors you have.

Consider Starbucks. In our opinion (as well as many others) Starbucks is a good example of a business that has created an authentic experience for their customers. There are many coffee houses across the country but none are quite as successful. That is because Starbucks has put in a tremendous amount of effort to make its locations the "third place," there is home, work, and Starbucks, a "destination" where people can have an experience they will remember, enjoy, and want to have again. They can read the paper while listening to good music, or sit and enjoy a delicious drink with a friend, or just relax and think in solitude. The staff is friendly, the environment is soothing, and the product is very good. Rather than just a sales transaction, buying coffee from Starbucks becomes an experience that the customer is unlikely to have anywhere else and one that they will want to have again.

How will you know, when you've struck the right chord with your customers? How important will that be to your business? If you know your customer, and respond to the tastes and needs of your target group, your customers will vote with their feet and your sales figures will reflect their enthusiasm.

In their article, "The Dance of Authenticity," Mathews and Wacker write that "Businesses can't declare themselves to be authentic, that's the customers' job," as well as, "authenticity might be the only sustainable competitive advantage" (2002, pp. 105–107).

In our view, truer words have never been spoken, nor more misunderstood by the world of business.

In fact, many companies talk about "authenticity" to their people and even list it as an advantage because they understand the immense power it holds. Many even attempt to create the impression through image advertising alone, believing it will be enough to carry them. They think they can fool the customer, but it doesn't take long before the customer catches on.

For example, in recent years, it's been common for financial services firms to advertise their integrity and pride in creating relationships that address the individual needs, goals of their customers, and trust. But have they, in fact, been real? Have they been successful? A look at the growing number of lawsuits and arbitration cases seems to indicate just the opposite: They have nearly tripled in the past year.

Too often, unfortunately, making the sale was valued more than meeting the customer's needs. It's well known, now, that the financial services industry has been rife with misleading analyses, conflicts of interest, backdoor deals, and other atrocities. In effect, customers were used for their money.

Authenticity? Hardly.

Because of that, it will be a long time before the financial services industry wins back the trust of the average investor it once enjoyed. These companies are forced (or choose to) rely on image advertising as a dressing that unfortunately won't do much to heal a devastating wound. Only years of better experiences of care and respect will promote the healing that is needed.

For example, Morgan Stanley is a very large financial services company that has had many well-documented questionable business practices as of late. These alleged unethical business practices have resulted in several multimillion-dollar settlements with the Securities Exchange Commission in which Morgan Stanley neither admits nor denies wrongdoing. So after all of this has taken place, what type of advertising does Morgan Stanley run? They run ads that depict their financial advisors as caring and empathetic and "embracing the dream of their client and making it their own" and so on. Many of their ads were over the top. One showed a man in the newborn section of the hospital and he was looking at one of the babies and talking about how she would have the best of everything and how he was going to make sure of that (the ad makes the viewer think that the man is her father). Then a bystander asks what her name is, and the man replies, "I don't know, let me check with her father, I am only their financial advisor." Touching, yes; but reality, no. It is exactly the opposite.

Another ad has a man making a toast to a newly married couple discussing his relationship with the bride and his pleasant wishes for the couple. This is very heart-felt and touching. Then after his toast is completed, he explains that he is only the financial advisor and now let's hear from her father. Does not seem quite right does it? When a company presents advertising that is so contrary to the reality of their business practices, two things become evident:

1. The ads are completely predictable based on what has happened to the company—the let's-make-people-think-we-did-not-do-what-we-did (or are still doing) mentality.
2. The company makes an assumption that consumers are stupid and that people will believe them if they just say that they did the opposite of what actually happened.

Morgan Stanley is not the only offender. Many companies (and people) follow the same pattern. Why do companies resort to simple image advertising rather than authenticity?

Good question. The answer: Authenticity is much harder. Wacker and Mathews point out that companies have a choice: To either carry "the burdens of authenticity or the comfort of anonymity." In other words, it takes a lot of work to create that experience for customers, to build that relationship and to genuinely care for them. It is much easier to just settle for being good enough, or not even really caring at all, if it gets you buy. In other words, just say "we do something," rather than actually do it.

Companies also have another important choice to make: Do they want to be responsible about how they conduct their business or do they want to take the attitude that things just happen to them? Arriving at the answer takes courage, because it entails taking a good, long, honest look in the mirror.

They must ask: Are we doing the right thing to win business? Are we having challenges because it is all too hard, everything is against us, it's all so unfair, and it is just too much to handle? Or, are we going to right our mistakes and create our own future?

The easy route is to do as your competitors do in the marketplace and let circumstances determine your success or try to fake your way through it. The more difficult, but far more rewarding road is to give the customer a real authentic experience and forge your own destiny. Remember, because the race of being successful never ends, you always have a chance to finish first. You simply must make the decision when to enter the race and how much you want to win it.

Now let's look at just how essential the human factor is to the proper sales approach and the authentic customer experience. We start with a look at technology and how companies are always trying to make everything more efficient and affective by incorporating more advanced technology. Companies always seem to ask, "What is out there that can help my business automate almost everything it does, so that it is optimally productive and optimally efficient"? In sales, what businesses associate with advancing their sales teams productivity is the use of customer relationship management (CRM) systems as the way to create long-lasting profitable relationships with customers.

This strikes us as odd for several reasons. First, the cost of CRM software system can be prohibitive—it can exceed more than $10's of millions and, in today's expense-conscious business environment, that can be a tough return on capital. Second, once installed, there are varying degrees of success with these systems, mostly because the data they collect can be very challenging to utilize. Third, many companies do not even have $1 million in annual sales. Fourth, and most importantly, viewing CRM as the solution to poor sales or declining sales directly overlooks the effect that the actual salesperson can have on improved productivity, provided that they are selling correctly.

Perhaps, the main reason CRMs are not the answer can be found in the article "The Better Half: The Artful Science of ROI Marketing, Strategy, and Composition" (Moeller, Mathews, and Rothenberg, 2003), which discusses, at length, the challenges of using a CRM:

> *Whether the customer is the customer or a business-to-business buyer, customer relationship management is fundamentally a human activity; technology can aid it, but it cannot substitute for it. (pp. 32–45)*

In other words, while software can help a company coordinate data on customer activity, the actual customer relationship depends on the person behind the sale. Successful selling is all about cultivating personal relationships.

In another article, "Avoid the Perils of CRM" (Rigby, Reichfeld, and Schefer, 2002) the previous point is further emphasized:

> *The CRM aligns business processes with customer strategies to build customer loyalty and increase profits over time.*

and

> *CRM can indeed do that but only after and we repeat, only after a traditional customer acquisition and retention strategy has been conceived of and implemented. (pp. 32–45)*

To see just how the human factor or sales process fits into that, let's look at some of the key phrases in these statements more closely:

- *Strategies to build customer loyalty:* This is what we have been discussing in previous pages: There is a need for a sales process to address customer loyalty right from the start of the customer relationship. The Golden Circle will do this by addressing the things that most concern customers from the very first interaction with a salesperson.

- *Increased profits over time:* This falls in place with the Golden Circle's goal of solidifying customer relationships, keeping customers connected to your business, and encouraging referrals, helping to ensure you and your business increase profits over time.
- *Traditional customer acquisition strategy:* This is a fancy term for sales and marketing. A customer acquisition strategy must incorporate a carefully chosen sales process that reflects every value of the customer.
- *Retention strategy:* This is where a CRM can have tremendous value because it organizes consumer information in ways that can be directly related to new sales or relationship-building opportunities. However, many customer retention factors are based on the initial quality of the sales process.
- *Conceived of and implemented:* This is the key and why we mention the subject of CRMs. As these articles point out, you need to have the right sales process in place first, before a CRM will add any value. And while a CRM may cost $1 million to $2 million, a good sales process can be examined for free.

CONCLUSION

Businesses need to take a close look to see how they can stand out from the rest of the marketplace. They can do that in several ways:

- By creating a better, more enjoyable, authentic or original experience for customers.
- By following good business practices that customers will respect and align with.
- By creating a positive sales experience between salesperson and customer, as if the salesperson were the customer's trusted, helpful neighbor.

Should you find glitches in your existing sales process, be sure to fix them as soon as you can. Once you do, you'll be on your way. No, you don't have to spend millions on high-tech software in order to make your selling work more effectively. In fact, as the Golden Circle demonstrates over and over, "the best things in business management are free."

Chapter 4

Sales Authenticity and Customer Connection

If we did as we should, we might have as we would.

—Scottish proverb

In our highly competitive, global marketplace, businesses need to make life as obstacle-free as possible for both customers and employees.

The Golden Circle was designed to enable a salesperson to connect with prospects strictly on the most fundamental of levels. When this is accomplished, a salesperson will have commonality with almost everyone he or she meets and be able to touch them with an approach that does not cause them to feel "sold" at all, but merely comfortable, appreciated, and well served—something the customer is not likely to experience elsewhere.

What are the things that all people share, and how can you incorporate those things into your sales approach? On the most basic of levels, everyone needs to eat, sleep, have shelter, and connect with family and friends. Everyone wants to be cared for and to care for other people, to feel good about him- or herself, to feel liked and appreciated, to be loved and to give love. And everyone, whether they admit it or not, likes to help other people.

Does that sound "soft" to you? Well, it is soft. Does that sound "simple" to you? Well, it is simple. The truth is we are all vulnerable human beings with some very common needs. Whether you're a janitor, a fisherman, a mechanic, an executive, a human resources manager, a hockey player, a stay-at-home mom (or dad), a politician, a movie star, or the check-out clerk at the grocery store, regardless of race or nationality at this simplest of levels, we are all alike, we understand and share one another's needs.

No matter how people may appear initially, remember that everyone has the same needs and values, and if you understand that, you can connect with anyone on that level. It is not something that you are going strike up a conversation about, "Hey, how's your value system these days?" It is something that you just know. And the more you work with people, with that in your mind and that guiding your actions, you will begin to develop a deeper appreciation for it. This will be visible to other people who work with you. Even though they may not be able to put their finger on it, they will know that there is "something about you that they feel comfortable with."

In sales, the experts tell us that when the customer comes in with a "need," we simply must fulfill that "need" to be successful. Part of that is true, generally a customer does have a need or they would not be out shopping for your service (unless they are compulsive shoppers). However, many companies "could" fulfill that customer's need, because many companies sell very similar products or services, which in reality, will all get the job done equally well. In that case, if you are just selling to fill that "need," you have not given yourself any advantage over your competitors; you did nothing profound that will set you apart.

Let's make something very clear as we dig deeper into the Golden Circle sales approach: We are *not* talking about the staid and trite, standard sales mantra that says, "People are motivated by fear, need, or excitement." There is a better way to connect with the emotional needs of customers. In a word, you need to show them that you care, and that your care is motivated by much more than the simple and selfish desire to sell them something.

Daniel Kahneman, a psychology professor at Princeton University, was awarded the 2002 Nobel Prize for economics for recognizing the importance of the emotional economy. In its announcement, the Royal Swedish Academy of Sciences cited Kahneman "for having integrated insights from psychological research into economic science, especially concerning human judgment and decision making under uncertainty." The Academy credited Kahneman for creating the basis for a new field of research.

What draws people to certain people? What causes people to feel better about working with one person or one business over another? Clearly, those companies who align their sales processes with universal customer values and emotions will be the ones who benefit. If you can communicate a genuine sense of shared values with current or prospective customers through communication and action, you will open the door to a trusting relationship. These highly valuable relationships with your customers and employees will drive your success. This is a fundamental step.

Secretary of State Colin Powell in a presentation on leadership once asked, "Have you ever noticed that people will personally commit to certain individuals who on paper (or on the chart) possess little authority, but instead possess pizzazz, drive, expertise, and a genuine caring for teammates and products?"

The same may be said for selling and salespeople. People want to feel genuinely regarded and will buy more frequently from salespeople who treat them with respect.

But how does that happen? You need to focus on customer values and expectations first then on the sale. If you learn to take a sincere interest and find out *who* each customer is and what matters to him or her, you will be well on your way.

In the sales process, there are six key ways to learn important information from your customers, knowledge that you can incorporate into conversations with them in subtle and insightful ways. They include:

1. Making comfort conversation.
2. Asking questions.
3. Learning personal insights about the prospect.
4. Having deep product knowledge.
5. Using commitment or closing actions correctly.
6. Being aware of your own "state of listening."

These tools will each be explained in detail. If you use these tools during customer contact, you will create a

complete transaction with your client that will lay a foundation that not only addresses the sale, but also creates a
meaningful relationship, even if the customer decides
not to buy.

You gain insight by making every effort to mentally
and emotionally stay with the client and read his or her
responses throughout the entire interaction. If the sales
transaction occurs in person, what does the prospect's
body language tell you? How engaged are the client's
questions or answers to your questions? Does he or she
seem apprehensive? Are the questions the client is asking
directed more toward your credibility or are they about
pricing and straightforward product information? Is the
prospect relaxed, bored, connected, alert, or disengaged?

Learning to be insightful is just about the most
important training any salesperson can have. It is fundamental to success because it helps you see and understand the transaction more effectively through the eyes
of the customer.

Making the effort to see the situation as the customer
does, allows you to anticipate, with a great degree of ac-
curacy, what the prospect wants and needs. This allows
the interaction to move along smoothly and without bar-
riers to communication.

Conversely, picture in your mind, the behavior of the
salesperson whose only care and intention is to get that
sale. What you most likely see is someone concerned
with controlling the conversation, leading the prospect

along through a preplanned sales outline and, in general, proceeding based only on his or her own objectives.

He or she may ask questions and appear to act with empathy and hide disinterest behind a smile. Even though the salesperson seems to be listening, he or she is really not hearing or working for the sake of the prospect. To this salesperson, the conversation leading up to the sale is only a formality one must go through to get the sale. No doubt, you've encountered salespeople like this. We all have. You know how it feels . . . not good at all.

Conducting sales transactions in this manner is the most common mistake that most salespeople and sales-driven companies do on a consistent basis. They follow the same sales routine without fail, whether it relates well to the client or not. They assume, mistakenly, that their results will improve just through two things: sticking more closely to "the system," and the sheer volume of contacts they make.

As a result, they never see the need, nor take the time, to look more closely at what really makes selling more effective. These salespeople and companies spend so much time and money trying to make the sale that they forget two things:

1. To make the most of each sales interaction in order to maximize the potential of current and future sales opportunities.

2. To make more of the sale than "just a sale"—in other words, set the foundation for the beginning of a relationship.

If a company's primary source of revenue is the sales process and the business does not close every sale, then it had better spend an equal amount of energy making sure that those who did not buy initially will want to buy in the future. (*Note:* We said will want to buy, not be chased down until they buy.)

"Making more of the sale" means that you have created an experience that is immeasurably better than the experience they would have had with any of your competitors.

The following are key ways to learn important information from your customers that you can use in every sales presentation. These guidelines will help to ensure that you cover everything that is important to your prospect, and that he or she is perceiving you correctly throughout the presentation.

Notice the levels of conversation that follow. Each must be treated with equal importance during any presentation, if possible. They are:

- *Comfort conversation:* That is, rapport building and establishing common ground. This can be about anything—the weather, a comment on a nice tie, the standard things you would talk about when you first meet anyone and want to make a connection. Comfort conversation is a good way to judge a prospect's mood.

- *Personal insights:* The salesperson skillfully asks about kids, pets, hobbies, future plans, work—anything that tells a little more about who the customer is and what his or her interests are. This information may be useful in the current transaction or in relationship building in the future. If you are genuinely interested, you will connect on the right level with the client quite naturally, and the answers you get will give you important insights. These questions can be asked at anytime during the sales process, they are no better at the beginning, the middle, or the end. The questions are best as long as they are used with every prospect, when they come naturally and when there is a sincere interest in the answers to those questions.

- *Fact-finding:* Through questions related to the customer's needs, a salesperson keeps things moving forward. The goal is not to control the conversation by using the questions to direct the prospect to a favorable conclusion about what you are selling or to get the prospect in that habit of saying yes. The goal is to learn what the prospect really wants, how you can help him get that, and how the customer prefers to be treated.

- *Product knowledge:* This means explaining the product or service in the most complete way possible and relating it to the customer's needs and desires. You need to be an expert about whatever it is you are selling. Not for the purposes of showing off your knowledge but because if you literally know everything about what you sell, you can more effectively help the prospect to get what they want from it.

- A *commitment or closing action:* Here, you are not necessarily asking for a credit card number, but instead, you want to help the customer to reach his or her own conclusion about the purchase. You put the answer right in front of the customer by means of indirect association. You do not ask for the commitment directly (at least not until the very end), but skillfully pull the prospect in that direction. You use phrases that give the customer several options that make him or her feel that the sale is appropriate. For example:
  - —"This may work for you."
  - —"This might be the best choice. Other customers have success with this option, and, based on what you have told me, this product (or service) seems the most logical choice."
  - —"You could make this work in your situation because your company has such-and-such."
  - —"This option would work nicely for you if you can do x, y, or z to make it successful."

By using indirect association, you won't be perceived as the "typical" assumptive salesperson, but rather as thoughtful, informative, honest, and concerned enough to meet the client's wants and needs, virtues that can open many doors.

Whenever you're beginning a sales presentation, be sure to work through these steps in the manner that is appropriate for the individual customer. In doing so, you'll increase your chance of getting a commitment. Leave one or more of these steps out, and you may not come across as well as you should.

For example, let's say you talk too long about product knowledge and your closing, and you spend little time with comfort conversation and personal insight questions, you may come across as entirely too aggressive and single-minded in your purpose.

Or, if you spend too much time with comfort conversation or on personal matters, the customer may perceive you as intrusive or unfocused. If you focus too much on personal information and your closing, the conversation may feel disruptive to the customer, because the two areas are extremes. Ramble on about product knowledge or in comfort conversation, and you may sound nice, but also indirect and unprofessional.

The key is to strike the right balance. You need to maneuver equitably through each of the levels during the initial customer interaction or presentation. By displaying superior product knowledge, helping the customer feel at ease, addressing a need and showing a sincere interest in the client, you create the perfect path to a successful sale and the beginning of a solid relationship.

CONCLUSION

To conclude, we'd like to emphasize that in any sales presentation, in any of these steps, the key is active, rather than passive, listening.

Think about it: If you are listening to someone and truly are interested in and focused on what they are saying, you will make your client feel important and cared about, an experience that any person highly values. On the phone, you will be sensitive to the client's tone of voice. In person, you will be attentive to their body language, all of which gives you valuable cues that will help you guide the conversation in the most appropriate way. Active listening will also give you a good read on how you are being perceived by that person.

If instead, you are listening in a lowered state of awareness, your client will pick up on that, and it will detract from any other effort you make to connect. It takes very little concentration or attention to listen to someone that way, and it also makes us all feel unimportant.

No doubt, you've had that experience yourself. When someone is not really listening, they tend to look around, to cut you off, to finish your sentences, and to jump in with their own replies instead of giving you a chance to offer your own. It is a very discouraging experience if you feel you have something important to say. And we all do.

Such inattentiveness prevents salespeople from coming across as genuine and creates an obstacle to any kind of bond with the customer. Poor listening shows insincerity and gives prospects the feeling that you are just waiting for them to finish talking so you can say whatever your sales technique calls for. This gives people a bad feeling, and salespeople a bad name. Instead, practice attentive listening; you will stand out as exceptional.

It would be worth your time for you and your colleagues or your employees to role-play through hypothetical sales scenarios, using effective listening as you incorporate each level of the presentation we have outlined in this chapter.

Be sure to have a discussion after each role-play session, where you respectfully critique one another and offer constructive suggestions and reactions to what you see and hear. What sounded natural and at ease, what did not? Consider repeating these sessions periodically, to prevent any omissions or bad habits from creeping in and thereby keeping the standard for your sales presentations high.

Once you and your sales team truly understand that this type of sales practice is the most effective and rewarding for all involved, then all of your efforts will be focused on both the short- and long-term selling needs of your company. Better still, you will now be giving each and every customer the experience that they deserve, that important *authentic* feeling that sets your team and business apart.

Chapter 5

Prospective Customer Service

Success in most things depends on knowing how long it takes to succeed.

—Baron de Montesquieu (1689–1755)

In the next four chapters, we examine the four main elements of the Golden Circle sales process—Prospective Customer Service, World-Class Care, Relationship, and Referral (Figure 5.1).

The first of these, Prospective Customer Service, is the transactional part of the sale—where the exchange of

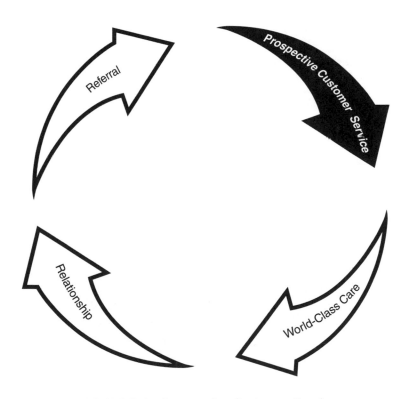

FIGURE 5.1 Prospective Customer Service

the product or service may take place. As we have discussed, since the initial interaction with a prospective
customer is so overwhelmingly important and affects a
potential long-term relationship with the customer, to
focus only on obtaining one sale from that interaction is
to undervalue it immensely.

That is why Prospective Customer Service concen-
trates on much more than just the sale. It is a way of
preparing for current and future sales at the same time. It
is a building process.

Keep in mind that the sales opportunity encompasses
several additional opportunities, including:

- Creating the most effective sales transaction possible.
- Once the sale is made, preparing the relationship for
  future, ongoing success.
- Should the sale not be made, leaving the person
  with a positive feeling, so he or she will want to
  come back and consider buying in the future, and
  will be inclined to recommend your business to others who may buy.

Everyone knows that a happy customer will tell a few
others of their experience and an unhappy customer will
tell his story to at least 20 other people. For that reason, it
is just as important to look at the cost of losing the sale as
it is to win the sale. If you don't create an advantage for
yourself in the marketplace every time you have any kind

of interaction with a customer, you are not working as effectively and productively as you could be.

We often wonder if most salespeople even consider the fact that they will never achieve a 100 percent closing rate. If you fail to think about how your customers will respond—whether or not they are pleased and connected or feel alienated when they decide not to buy—then, over time, the law of averages will easily affect the profitability of your business in a negative way.

It takes about four good sales experiences to make up for every bad one. Think carefully of what that really means: Every time someone says something bad about your business (or you as a salesperson), 20 people either don't buy from you or will have reservations before they do. To make up for those 20, you need four happy customers to each drive in five new sales, just to net out the effect of having one unhappy customer.

Why would you want to work in such an obviously unproductive manner? Why waste so much time, money, and effort?

Prospective Customer Service is essentially the art of positively affecting every aspect of the sale, no matter how subtle, from the very beginning. Its goal is to set the proper foundation for a relationship with the customer, over and above making a sale.

This is an extremely important paradigm shift for any sales-driven company. The reason? Any salesperson can smile and establish rapport throughout the duration of the sale. This is mediocre order taking or scrambling for business. Very little skill, initiative, effort, or training is required. Simple order taking does nothing to ensure that you will win future business from the customer. Nor, does it mean that the customer will feel loyal to you in any way, once the sale has been made.

However, if instead, you are genuinely concerned and sincerely interested in your customer, your honest interest will make a dramatic difference in the customer's experience and result in increased revenues. What is required is caring enough to try a little harder with every customer, and doing so consistently, until a relationship starts to take hold.

Creating this healthy, relationship-building customer experience requires skill, planning, and certain sales personality traits. Although the process can be taught effectively, people who naturally show care and concern in other areas of their lives will understand the process intuitively, which makes a big difference.

You also need to create a healthy, employee-centered business environment for this type of sales system to flourish. The fact is, caring, highly motivated, customer-oriented salespeople will not stay with a company for long if they are not being treated well themselves.

There are three reasons for this:

1. Customer-oriented salespeople will want to keep a positive attitude toward even the most demanding or

difficult customers. This is harder when salespeople do not feel good about the company or about their own jobs.
2. Customer-oriented salespeople will want to sell only products and services they believe in. Salespeople must feel good about what they sell if they hope to be able to deliver good results over the long term.
3. Customer-oriented salespeople understand the value of their approach, so they know they can get jobs elsewhere.

The whole idea behind Prospective Customer Service is to give your customers an experience that is rare; something they're not likely to receive anywhere else. That's important, because today's consumers are prone to comparison-shopping, and they can easily do so by using the Internet. The increased savvy and expectations of your customers should indicate that you need to draw your customers in and keep them; otherwise, you may easily lose their business to your competitors.

In the business of selling today, what matters is whether or not you and the company hit your budget, not what your closing ratio is. So why use your closing ratio as a measure of sales success? You could have a 90 percent closing ratio and not make your budget and conversely you could have a 10 percent closing ratio and hit it.

Realistically, your first-time closing ratio is likely to be 30 to 40 percent. If you sell big-ticket items or to corporations, it will probably be 10 percent to 20 percent.

That means (depending on what you sell) 60 percent to 90 percent of your customers will not buy the first time they sit down with you. In that case, you need to make sure the overwhelming majority of the customers who contact your business buy "in due time." Your goal should be to capture more of the market—more than your competition—at some point down the line in a consistent manner. Keep in mind that just because a prospect did not buy from you does not mean they did not buy the product. They just bought what they wanted somewhere else from someone else, and you lost that business.

The only way to consistently hit your budgeted sales numbers is to make the customer experience "authentic" for each and every one of your customers. We can't, of course, tell you exactly how to do that. Authenticity, by definition, will be different for each customer. But we can tell you it will boost your success rate dramatically if you do it right. The better you become at distinguishing yourself from the competition, the better off you and your business will be.

As we discussed in Chapter 4, authenticity can't be faked. For the most part, customers are able to see through image advertising. True authenticity allows customers to feel that they are being treated genuinely, regardless of what they are being sold.

There is nothing like the real thing. Customers need to be drawn to a product or service for good reasons, then presented and closed in the same fashion consistently, with care and respect. Treat customers this way and your business will have good labels, such as "out of the ordinary," and "really different."

The reason that you need an authentic experience to create a strategic advantage for you in the marketplace is that consumers are constantly bombarded with so many choices—5 different wireless phone companies, 30 car dealers, scores of real estate companies, dozens of software companies, 20 department stores, 12 furniture stores, 50 financial service firms, and so on.

Yet, so many businesses conduct business the same way. Companies may run different ads in an effort to establish a unique image or identity, but really, most are the same. They may pretend or say that they are different, but only offer mediocre sales and customer service transactions.

This is your huge opening, your awaiting niche, your grand opportunity to stand out.

Just treat people the way they like to be treated, and you will be different. Why? Because the majority of sales training that is done these days is still based on one of two things:

1. Tired sales principles that were developed long ago; or
2. The hottest, the newest, fanciest trend.

But therein lies the opportunity. Few consumers are fooled, dazzled, or even pleased by these approaches any more. And it is not like a salesperson cannot be pegged from a mile away, people are so alert to salespeople, it is as though they can almost smell them as they get closer. This means the door is wide open for you to walk in with the right approach, and stay with your customer.

Salesmanship has been so bad for so long that just being a salesperson stacks the deck against all of us from the start. Salespeople are generally regarded as self-serving and chameleon-like, or much worse. Nobody really looks forward to meeting the salesperson and "being sold." Which is why you may see many books or articles that say it is all about *not* selling people, it's all about servicing, or it's all about being nice, or it's all about being anything but a salesperson. That's because the pendulum always swings from one end all the way to the other, one extreme to the next and rarely does it land squarely in the middle. Many people may vilify salespeople, but the fact is that salespeople have to sell. There is absolutely no way around it and nothing wrong with selling to people. One good thing about the years of salespeople doing things the wrong way is that consumers are so conditioned to salespeople's actions that they are at least prepared to be sold to when they meet a salesperson. You must be proud of being a salesperson (we are), sell the right way to people and no one will fault you for selling to them.

This whole stereotype of a salesperson has come about from the many years of salespeople doing just what they were taught to do: Get the transaction, get the money. For years, many of the so-called *best* salespeople and sales trainers taught salespeople to go after what they want for themselves, rather than to think of the customer. That is the one big perplexing conundrum about the profession of selling.

For example, if you are in sales, you might recall the patented, usual methods used to make a sale, such as "if I could . . . would you," "sharp angle closes," "circling the wagons," or "tie downs." All of these are effective to a degree, but are single-mindedly designed to get the buck.

These techniques amount to manipulation. They come across as insulting and offensive to consumers because salespeople have been using and abusing these techniques and many others that revolve around the same premise for 30 years.

Not only that, when a prospect fails to buy, salespeople have been taught to put the name in a "cold lead file" and recycle them again and again, until the prospect either buys something or tells the harassing salesperson to leave him alone. This type of negative selling only widens the chasm between a salesperson and the customer as well as the gap between the customer and the business for which the salesperson works. Negative selling rarely builds a relationship.

Negative selling by our definition is any sales approach that does not first and foremost seek to satisfy the customer and firmly set the stage for a long-term relationship.

It becomes a "push" sales approach rather than a "pull" sales approach. It tends to drive customers and salespeople farther apart (because it is one-sided), rather than bringing them closer together. There is little benefit for the customer in this type of sales approach.

Another example (and there are many) of a process that has been mistakenly associated with effective selling is *neurolinguistic programming* that, simply stated, calls for creating a sense of commonality with the customer by mimicking his or her movements and using similar gestures or voice inflections.

Neurolinguistic programming cannot and should not be the basis for creating the ideal sales system. The reason: It does not focus on being genuinely concerned for the customer. Instead, it focuses on making the prospect feel that the salesperson is the same as the prospect, in order to get the prospect to lower his or her defenses and allow communication to flow more freely. This creates a false sense of trust and comfort. The salesperson's objective is to then influence the sale with this so-called "trust."

While neurolinguistic programming may seem well intentioned, when applied as a sales system it is just another form of manipulation. (It was originally developed as a study in organizational behavior, not as a sales system.)

Trust cannot and should not be manipulated or created as the "impression" of trust, it must be earned over time. Otherwise it is not really *trust*. And it should never be misused for the salesperson's gain. This process is wrong-headed because, in fact, it is not real. There are hundreds of other nonauthentic sales techniques that have attempted to put the spin on how to sell. Each and every one is tilted more toward the salesperson than the customer, and that is the disconnect.

Opposite to this is the sales system that is designed to bring the salesperson and customer closer together and keep them that way, the "pull" sales objective, as we have mentioned. The ideal sales system focuses on real and genuine feelings and emotions, such as learning about your customer's family, job, interests, or anything else that is important to them. In other words, it focuses on finding out *who* your customer is.

The problem is that most salespeople never take the time to find out who the customer is, nor are they genuinely interested. That's because too many salespeople have had the wrong training, which in turn, slows down earning potential, negatively affects employee turnover, and reduces the profitability of the business. It also perpetuates the sales profession's bad name.

Learning "real" things about the customer helps build trust, establishes common ground, and shows the customer that you are interested in them as human beings and not just for their money, which is the right way to begin a customer relationship. Genuine care and concern tends to disable a person's defenses in a very positive manner. Treat customers this way and, at a minimum, the customer will give you the chance to be measured on your own merits without the barrier of the salesperson stereotype getting in the way. Then, the sale process can move forward in a more comfortable manner for both parties. No sense of pressure to close the sale on the part of the salesperson and no sense of anxiety (wondering about the intentions of the salesperson) on the customer side. This allows the process to flow much more naturally.

Again make no mistake: The need to close sales and hit the budget is essential to any business no matter what sales system it uses. However, anyone who preaches the value of aggressive and controlling sales techniques or, at the other end of the spectrum, the cozy, coddling sales approach does not understand the business of consistent sales success. The only thing these techniques do is lead to a transaction of some sort. That's it, good or bad, depending on your definition. Maybe a sale, maybe a relationship, but rarely both. Sales cannot flow consistently, without both a sale and a relationship happening all the time.

When you have salespeople who know that the most important part of making a sale is to create trust and show a sincere interest in the customer, then you can be confident that your business will always be represented in a positive, appropriate manner. You will also know that your sales efforts are now compounding all of the time because of the collective action of relationship building by your salespeople.

Now let's say you do get your salespeople to take the positive approach and adopt the principles of Prospective Customer Care. The truth is, no matter how positive that first interaction with a customer is, it will still take time for the customer to truly and fully trust your salesperson. You can only hope to open the door on the first interaction, to help the customer see that the salesperson and the business are different from the stereotype. Salespeople will only win trust if they display the same genuine concern and interest on a *consistent and predictable basis with the customer.* It's not all about how that first meeting goes, it's not about the "close," it is about what happens every single time a salesperson sees the customer or potential customer whether they bought something or not. No matter if it happens in the grocery store or at the veterinarian's office, the communication must be exactly as it was when you where selling to them, genuine, sincere, and real. If it is not, then the salesperson exposed his true self and his true intentions and it is off to the races for the customer to tell their friends. Every single time a prospect or customer is seen, it needs to be viewed as another opportunity to improve that customer's opinion of you and the business, whether you are at work or not. Why would someone be any different at work than how they really are? (Don't answer that!) Consistency is the only thing that can really build customer trust or trust in general for that matter. Consistency takes time.

Creating this consistent customer experience is what will keep you honest and force you to see this sales culture change all the way through. To use physical fitness as an analogy, it is a little like looking at yourself naked in the mirror. You can cover up to make yourself look more fit, put on a slick suit or a nice dress, but you will never look the way you want until you start doing the right things and do them consistently, that is, like exercising and eating right. But once you go through all that and see what you like in the mirror (naked), you will feel good about it and you won't want to return to your old habits.

Similarly, once you have established a genuine and authentic feel about your selling, you can never go back, and truthfully, you won't want to. Why would you?

Prepare yourself: It will be hard to get customers to discover that you and your sales process are different from many others. However, once you create an exceptional and original experience for your customers, you will be miles ahead of your competition.

Follow that up with proper training, proper management, and intelligent financial acumen, and your business can't lose.

Once you start this process, it will create its own momentum. The Golden Circle Prospective Customer Care process works from the most basic of human values, values that are universal to all of us. So, eventually, as you will see, it will all come to you very naturally.

Chapter 6

World-Class Care

If honesty did not exist, we ought to invent it as the best means of getting rich.

—Honore Gabriel Riqueti Mirabeau
(1749–1791)

World-Class Customer Care allows you to continue to build on the foundation of trust and goodwill to ensure that a good relationship with your customers is sure to follow. At most companies (including your competitors), customer service is usually the next step after the sale. That is, if the company wants to make some effort at keeping at least some of its customers.

Generally, people expect customer service to include things such as taking care of their concerns about a product or service they have purchased, fixing a billing issue, or taking a return on unwanted or faulty merchandise. And, they expect it to be done in a timely manner with courtesy and a smile. Businesses who handle customer matters in this way are perceived as reputable. If they do anything less, customers will label them as poor risks and walk away, spreading the word about their dissatisfaction in the process.

Consider this example: Two friends were discussing furniture purchases. One of them had just bought a condominium, and the other had moved into a new apartment. The new condo owner had considered purchasing furniture from a well-known department store, but heard that someone else had purchased some coffee tables, and had to send them back three times because they arrived scratched. This department store carried the furniture at attractive prices.

However, this potential, new customer not only bought somewhere else because of the negative word-of-mouth about the store, but she passed on the information to her friend, who may have been another potential customer.

The second friend purchased an office desk at a popular casual furniture store. Unfortunately, the desk the store delivered was defective. This friend called the store at once, and that same afternoon, a new desk arrived, free-of-charge, in perfect condition.

The store staff, working as a team, also treated this customer with understanding, responsiveness, and courtesy throughout the whole process. As a result, the second woman became a frequent customer and relates her positive experience and recommends the store to anyone who expresses an interest in purchasing furniture (Figure 6.1).

In the first instance, the large department store provided typical customer service; it addressed a problem three times and finally delivered, but caused the customer anger and frustration in the process.

In the second case, the store provided World-Class Care. There was a problem, but it was rectified deftly and properly, with empathy for the customer's position. The store staff listened, rectified the matter in a very upbeat, "no problem" manner that caused her little or no inconvenience. As a result, the second woman is now developing a relationship with that store.

Which business do you think will fare better, in the end? Customer service is necessary to keep any business

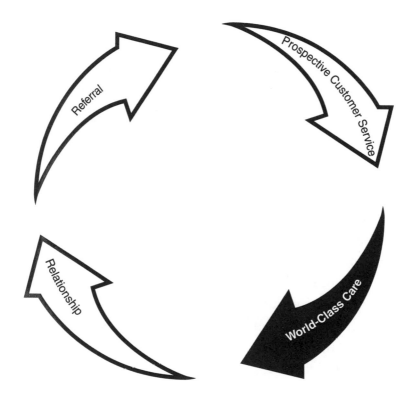

FIGURE 6.1 World-Class Care

alive. But in today's competitive climate, just providing typical good customer service is not enough for a business to thrive. Instead, you need to make World-Class Care your mission. There is a distinct difference.

The reason: Inevitably, someone will come along and deliver your product or service just as well and at a lower cost. In this case, your customers will leave if you have not established a genuine relationship with them. However, customers will remain loyal if your relationship with them is strong even if a competitor can offer the same product or service less expensively. And they will even refer others to your business on the basis of that relationship.

Which brings us to the story of Jessie, the Chesapeake Bay Retriever. This story illustrates how you must take care of your customers and protect them so your competitors do not take them.

We had lost one of our family dogs (we had two) of many years, Sammi. She passed away and we had waited a number of months before looking for another family pet to keep our other dog company. We finally made the decision to start looking for a new family dog and went to the local Animal Shelter to start our search.

The first trip was not a success even though we looked at (and walked) a number of dogs, they just weren't what we were looking for and I guess we still hadn't really gotten over the loss of Sammi. A month or so later, the second trip was more successful. We went back and met (and walked) a number of dogs. Several of them were just too young and energetic, some where not good with other animals, and we wanted to leave one puppy for one of the families there that day with a child. So we were getting a little discouraged. The counselor suggested that we meet Jessie, a Chesapeake Bay Retriever who was about six years old at the time. We knew nothing about Chessies, that is the nickname for them, but we were about to find out in a hurry.

The counselor said that she had been with a family of young children but they could no longer care for her so they gave her to the shelter. She had been placed with two other owners previously but it just didn't work out. We asked what was wrong and the counselor said that she was very protective and did need to have an area that she could call her own. That did not sound that bad, so we gave her a try, put her on a leash and took her for a walk. She did fine. We asked the counselor if she got along with other dogs and were told that Chesapeakes are okay with other dogs but they do stay pretty much to themselves. We asked because our other dog Bruiser was a big, 160-pound, mixed-breed sheep dog and wolfhound. We wanted to make sure that they would not have a problem socializing. So after some discussion, we agreed to take Jessie back home to meet Bruiser to see if they would get along.

The first meeting was fine, Jessie met Bruiser and they seemed to get along. We were very pleased since Jessie was just the right age and was not a dog that jumped all over you or your guests. Since we were pretty encouraged with this first meeting, we adopted her. Bruiser and Jessie seemed to be getting along fine, no altercations. However, once Jessie noticed that Bruiser had some dog toys that he frequently neglected, things changed.

Chesapeakes have apparently been bred to retrieve, protect, and guard the waterfowl that hunters shoot until the hunter comes to get them. So while Bruiser was outside one day, Jessie's natural instincts took over and she went over to Bruiser's neglected pile of toys and "retrieved" every one of them and brought them over to her dog bed. Once Jessie had all the toys in her possession, she watched over them very attentively.

A little while later Bruiser returned, eventually discovering that all of his toys were gone. Jessie made it perfectly clear that these toys were now hers. After encountering Jessie's determination to keep the toys once or twice, Bruiser retreated to his bed. When Jessie went outside for a stroll around the yard, Bruiser went over to her area and took back only one toy. Upon her return, Jessie immediately noticed that this toy was missing and as soon as Bruiser got up and moved away, she promptly took it back. Eventually, we had to buy Bruiser another toy and Jessie was fine with that. As long as it wasn't one of hers, apparently he could keep it.

Be like a Chesapeake Bay Retriever with your customers. Take care of them, protect them, and guard them. The time, energy, and money you invest in getting your customers in the first place requires you to make sure that once you have them, they stay with you. This is only done by keeping in touch and making sure you that you have an outstanding commitment to them. Only then can you feel confident that they are protected from being "retrieved" by another company. By the way, we still have Jessie and she still takes care of her toys.

But how do you create that relationship? World-Class Care is about trying to make your customers feel as if they "belong" with you and your business, and reinforcing that feeling every time they deal with you.

While these things sound small, you must create the atmosphere of community. Silly as it may sound, you must create a warm place, where people feel welcome and part of the group, "where everybody knows your name," as the television show *Cheers* slogan went. To take this lightly would be a sorry mistake, because this is exactly what people want.

While it's true that doing so takes extra effort, you will be willing to make that effort if creating a relationship with your customers is important to you, and your customers will sense this feeling. If you are interested in the customer as a person rather than "just a sale," you'll naturally ask questions.

In the initial interaction, you'll learn the basics, such as what they are looking for, how much they'd like to spend, how they want to use the product or service, and perhaps, where they live and how they found out about your business.

But if you really care about the customer and use the approach we suggest in Chapter 4, you'll find out many more important things, that is, what the customer likes and dislikes, whether or not he or she has a family, if they have children or pets, what they like to do for fun, if they enjoy their job, even what their future goals may be.

You'll be amazed at how much you can learn about someone in three minutes if they feel that you're really interested in them. People love to talk about themselves; they often need the emotional outlet. And you need to love to listen to them.

The best way to provide excellent World-Class Care, and build loyalty, is to remember all of those "little" things about your customers. Remembering and relating them back to your customers works like pure magic.

Not only that, it's inexpensive. It doesn't take a lot of time, nor a $1 million to $2 million customer relationship management (CRM) system, as we discussed in Chapter 3. It is just takes salespeople and employees who care enough to take a genuine interest in knowing their customers.

Whenever a customer walks in the door, or whenever you speak with a customer on the phone, be sure to focus the conversation on that customer from the start. Start with some comfort conversation or personal questions. Start with, "How is your daughter's basketball going?" or "How are you doing with your new job?" Let them know that they are your number one priority, and then move on to business matters.

Do this, and as a rule, you will connect with your clients in a real way. Because this type of personal connection is so unusual in this rather impersonal, technological society we live in, people will appreciate it. And we guarantee that you'll find yourself enjoying your job much more as well.

The effect of caring for someone or of being cared for is so powerful because it reminds us all of family, of community, and of belonging. Make your customers feel that they belong in some way, and they will stick with you, and they will tell others how special and unique your company is. You can't script or put a price on that kind of word-of-mouth marketing. You need to make a constant corporate effort to establish some type of emotional connection with your customers.

In a speech given by Howard Schultz, founder of Starbucks (2002, 24-Hour-Fitness Convention), he cited a fact that we found very interesting. He mentioned that between 1963 and 2003 consumer confidence and believability in corporate advertising has dropped by 83 percent. In other words, over the past 40 years, people have stopped believing the ads they see.

Why is that? Because advertising has become lip service, too many companies say they focus on their customers, but their actions prove just the opposite. They do little or nothing to connect with their customers. They're focused, instead, on the simple sales transaction. They'd rather take the money for themselves and run. The spate of corporate scandals that we've seen lately is shameful evidence of this selfishness and greed. How will American business ever win back the trust and confidence of American consumers, not to mention employees? That's what we mean when we say following a sales system that just focuses on how to create a transaction is like buying a house without rooms, a transaction on its own is hollow. A transaction that is designed to be the beginning of a sincere relationship is complete.

Eighty-eight percent of clients indicate that their confidence is either somewhat lessened or greatly lessened in accounting firms and mutual funds corporations due to the many recent scandals and irregularities (*Accounting Today*, 2004). That's a lot. How long do you think it will take for the financial services industry to completely rebuild consumer confidence?

How long do you think it will take for all of us to gain back the trust of the 88 percent of consumers that don't believe the ads they see?

You can create trust in your business step-by-step, with each customer contact you have. In this environment, the smallest details become all the more important.

Think about the huge advantage you could give yourself and your business if you do make that genuine connection with your customers and become known for it in your marketplace. The difference in sustainable profits will be substantial. The difference in your own personal satisfaction will be tremendous.

So give the customer an authentic experience, a real experience. No fluff, nothing but the real deal. That "naked person in the mirror," the so-called transparent interaction, is what customers today really want. And they want it every time.

Chapter 7

Relationship

Practice does not make perfect, it makes permanent.

—Floyd Wickman,
real estate trainer and mentor

There is one, very important thing we'd like to emphasize when it comes to the relationship you have with your customer: It is something you must actively cultivate on a continuing basis. It is not something that you can assume you have—unless you want to put it in jeopardy. Assuming that you have a relationship with your customer is understandable. However, such passivity is exactly the reason that most businesses fail to successfully maintain many of the newer relationships they have with their customers. Figure 7.1 shows the importance your relationship with your customer plays in the Golden Circle.

Many companies do what it takes in terms of staff training and customer interaction to develop some level of a connection with customers in the process of a sale. But once a sale is complete, they mistakenly conclude that nothing else is necessary. They believe that, once they are formed, these relationships are permanent. As a result, in many cases they lose valuable customers to competitors.

And that is a shameful waste, indeed.

The fact is that both business and customer relationships require constant attention and effort. In our own personal lives, only the relationships we have born of long histories can endure long periods of little or no interaction. Like that childhood friend that you went to school with for 12 years. You don't speak with or see that friend for years, yet when you reconnect, you manage to pick

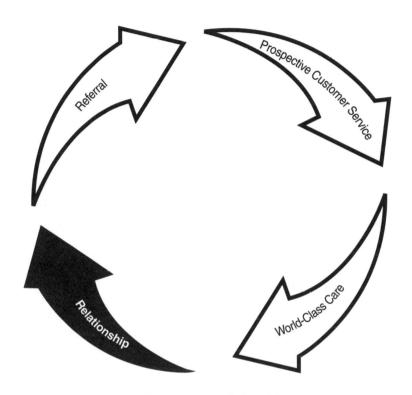

FIGURE 7.1   Relationship

things up where you left off. The primary reason you can do that is because you have 12 years of shared, day-to-day experience.

Relating this to your customer base, if you make no regular effort to build stronger relationships, you will keep an extremely small percentage of your customers—hardly enough to maintain good profit levels. If your goal is healthy profits, you have to create a history of good service and positive experiences with your customers. Then and only then can you have even a little confidence that your customers will be fairly well insulated from your competitors.

Clients need contact monthly, from a familiar voice, someone to check in just to see how it is going. You can also send them handwritten notes, or just drop by to say hello. Your customer will value anything you do that requires effort and a personal touch—provided, of course, your goal really is to stay in touch and not to sell them something else. The things we mentioned earlier—e-mail, mass-mailers, having others make the call—are customer contact tools. The problem is, they are not personal, and as a result, are not valued as highly by your customers.

Let us use another physical fitness analogy. Let's say that you work for months, or even years, to reach a personal fitness goal. You experience firsthand, just how much time, determination, discomfort, and overall effort it takes to reach that goal. As well as the supreme satisfaction of having reached it.

But you're there, you've done it, so you stop exercising. You begin to take your fitness for granted. Before you know it, you start to lose ground and realize that some of the gains you have made are disappearing quickly. You realize if you stop exercising and make no effort at all to maintain your fitness level, you'll lose nearly everything you gained and find yourself nearly at the same point at which you started.

The same is true with the relationships you have with your customers. Just like exercising, building a solid relationship with your customers requires time and consistent effort. You need to do a lot of things to earn their trust and goodwill.

It can take months or sometimes even years, but every one of those relationships will be well worth every minute of time put into it as the years go by. Once you have reached a level of trust and have a relationship with your customers, you must do everything possible to keep that relationship going and growing so you can enjoy the benefits for years to come. Otherwise, you may lose it and find yourself nearly at the same point at which you started.

Growing relationships means continuing to improve the opinion of you and your business held by the customer—something you can do with every interaction. Think of it as climbing a staircase, every positive interaction gets you one step closer to the top with that particular customer.

You must also avoid one very common mistake: ignoring, and perhaps neglecting, your current customers in favor of new ones. Unfortunately, both novice and seasoned salespeople may often see their new customers as more important. Or worse, some treat the customer on the phone as more important than the customer waiting or sitting in front of them. It's just a matter of courtesy, and understanding how impatient we all are these days.

You need to strike a balance and give your customers equal consideration.

Never forget that the longer you keep a customer, the more satisfied, comfortable, and accustomed to you and your company they will become. Along with that satisfaction comes a powerful endorsement and a referral every time they tell someone else about your business and that is *what selling for today and planning for tomorrow is all about.* Let us share with you a story about thinking ahead.

In Maine as in many other New England states around the middle of September, many farm stands pop up where people go to get their pumpkins and a number of other seasonal decorations. These stands also offer a variety of seasonal produce. The stands are quaint and beautiful because all the leaves are starting to turn. They are also fun to visit with the family so it is very common to see many families out together picking their favorite pumpkin to bring home.

One particular cool, late September morning at a local farm stand, we saw a little girl and her father walking hand in hand. As we neared the stand, we noticed that the little girl had a dollar bill clutched in her left hand. She stood in front of the stand and studied the pumpkins with great care. The pumpkin stand was arranged with the very large and impressive pumpkins on the left, then as you moved to the right, the pumpkins got smaller (and less expensive) all the way down to the end

of the stand where the very inexpensive and strange looking gourds were arranged.

The little girl looked at each pumpkin on the stand
and then went over to the farmer and said, "Hi, I'm here
to buy the biggest pumpkin I can." He smiled and said,
"That's good, we have a lot of very big pumpkins." She
then showed him the dollar bill and asked what she could
get for "that much money." The farmer frowned a little
(as if he knew he had to disappoint her) and he took her
over to the dollar pumpkins, which were really the
gourds. They were very small and funny looking and you
could see the disappointment on the face of the little girl.
She looked at the farmer and asked, "Only these are a
dollar?" The farmer nodded. She put her hand on her
chin, visibly sad, looked at her dad and then said to the
farmer, "Can we go into the pumpkin patch?" (which
was right behind the farm stand), "There may be a
pumpkin I can buy for a dollar in there that is bigger than
these." Wanting not to completely disappoint the little
girl, the farmer said, "Okay."

Off they went into the field, the farmer, the little girl,
and her dad. She was still clutching the dollar bill as she
walked through the rows looking at the pumpkins. The
farmer led them over to one section where the pumpkins
where all very small and kind of green (because they were
not fully ripe). She spotted one and said, "Can I buy that
for a dollar?" It was a pretty good-sized pumpkin but it was
solid green. She studied it for a moment and then said,

"No, the stem is not right." She continued on and soon she spotted another green pumpkin, looked at it and said, "Can I buy this one for a dollar"? The farmer said, "Okay." She again studied it very carefully and finally said, "No, it doesn't have the right shape." Off, they went again looking for the perfect pumpkin, with the farmer growing a little impatient. Suddenly, she stopped, pointed to a good-sized green pumpkin with a perfect shape and asked, "Can I buy that one for a dollar?" The farmer thought for a second and then said, "Okay, that's fine." He took out a small knife to cut the pumpkin from the stalk and the little girl said, "No, don't cut it off, I will be back in October to pick it up." Then she handed the farmer her dollar bill. The farmer smiled, took the dollar bill, looked at her father who had a big grin on his face, and said "That is one clever young lady." The two came back in October and the little girl got her big, perfect pumpkin, the farmer got his dollar, and they both had a story to tell.

The point of this true story is that in many sales organizations selling becomes a trade off; take what you can get today (in the short term), at the expense of tomorrow, and it doesn't have to be like that. Most companies (and salespeople) either knowingly or not, put themselves into that "trade off" position based on the way they have been doing things in the past. Not selling the right way, failing to look at the broader picture, and rarely planning for the future. If you want consistent sales success, you must do all three of those things all the time.

Just as important to remember is that if you lose a long-time customer for lack of contact, their distaste for your company will be powerful. They may very likely feel that the relationship they had with you was really about nothing but money—that you've gotten what you wanted from them, so they are of no more value to you. If you allow this to occur, you can be assured that they will find a way to tell many more than 20 people and it will take many more than four good sales to make up for losing that one customer.

Remember: The things that will keep your relationships strong with your customers are the same things that won you the relationship in the first place. Don't change your strategy or play the game differently after you have any kind of relationship with your customer, new or old.

To use another analogy from the world of health and fitness: We have all heard about "quick fix" weight loss products—pills, gels, fad diets, and so on. Most don't work; they only give the impression of weight loss. They exploit the customer's hope. And if some people seem to take off weight temporarily, the method is generally very unhealthy. You can bet that those pounds will come back because the basics of healthy weight loss have been completely ignored.

The same is true if a salesperson is trained in ways to give customers the "impression of being cared for," rather than really caring for customers, the relationship that develops will be based on a lie, to put it bluntly. As a result, it will never last.

A business can only build strong relationships with customers by teaching their salespeople how to be genuinely concerned for their customer base all the time. That's it; there is no alternative.

Even if you work for a very large company, such as Wells Fargo, IBM, Costco, or Fed Ex, you may think it's impossible to consistently deliver the correct message and values to your customers.

You are wrong. Even if your company has 150,000 employees and 20 million customers, great relationships can still be had with every one of those customers.

The reason is simple: Everything that needs to happen in any large organization can and invariably will be achieved, if the goal is valued highly enough.

While none of us is a fan of the IRS, it is true that this huge agency was given the mandate by Congress to become more streamlined and become more customer-friendly, and they did.

Delivery companies have constantly increased value-added services, such as package tracking and instant signature verification, just to have an edge on their competitors.

High-technology companies constantly need to work around newly introduced disruptive technologies.

Hundreds of companies have diversified their revenue lines to compensate for economic challenges that have threatened their standard revenue models.

If any of these businesses can change their ways, then so can you. And so can your company. If building and maintaining genuine, long-lasting customer relationships is important to you, you'll do it. And you'll profit from the greater personal satisfaction and higher revenues that those relationships bring.

Chapter 8

Referral

I not only use all the brains I have but all I
can borrow.

—Woodrow Wilson (1856–1924)

We devote this chapter to the importance of customer referral because treating customers respectfully in the referral process is vital to maintaining good relationships with them.

Referrals (Figure 8.1) must not be taken for granted by any means—even when the customer's buying experience has been very positive. Referrals must be handled carefully and deftly, and initiated at the most appropriate moment. You must use some sophistication when asking for referrals.

Unfortunately, most people see salespeople as *takers*, even though customers receive a product or service for their money. As a result, if you ask a customer for a referral immediately after they make a purchase, it will take away from their moment of feeling good and special about their purchase and quickly turn the focus to what you want from them.

This instantly lowers a customer's sense of worth and importance because only moments ago, they gave you their money and their business, and now you are, however, indirectly asking them for something else and making it about you.

Truly successful selling will reverse the flow—and change that stereotypical dynamic from *taking* to *giving*.

If, immediately after a sale, you ask someone for a referral as a mandated aspect of the sales process, it is *taking*. If, instead, you let a customer know how much you

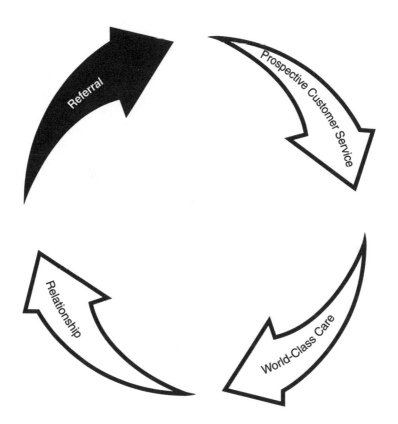

FIGURE 8.1   The Four Steps to the Golden Circle: Prospective Customer Service, World-Class Care, Relationship, and a Properly Handled Referral

appreciate their business, walk them to the door, send them a thank-you note and consistently follow up with them, that is *giving*.

Good businesses are built on customer goodwill and repeat business. Don't try to rush it. Neither you nor your company can expect to be overly successful from the start. We all saw what happened with those "overly successful" Internet bubble companies. You and your company must earn that success with the four steps we have been talking about: with Prospective Customer Service, World-Class Care, good Relationships, and properly handled Referrals. It will take time to become a truly good salesperson—one who is genuinely liked by customers and who meets or exceeds budgeted numbers consistently. Successful salespeople, in turn, will help to build successful companies over time.

Of course, you need to trust your own judgment: If asking for a referral at the end of the transaction seems appropriate, then go for it! Or, if a referral is willingly offered, then accept it! Just be sure to remind yourself that selling cannot be purely and blatantly transactional—you need to build a relationship before asking your customer for anything at all. It is your responsibility.

Now, some diehard sales "know-it-alls" will insist that, by not asking for a referral right away, you are wasting valuable time and unnecessarily elongating the sales process of another potential lead because the customer is most excited just after the sale has been made.

Their argument is that, in this state of excitement, the customer will be most willing to give the name of a friend or relative for you to call. Because of this, you should take full advantage of that excitement and secure a referral.

This is pretty true to form for the typical salesperson. We understand why some people might think this way; it's the easiest thing to do. However, if they were to really examine the sales process closely, they would see the wisdom in building personal and product value before requesting a referral.

By pushing point-of-sale referrals too much, many companies lose customers and find themselves eventually turning over their markets unnecessarily and decreasing their sales productivity levels. That's especially true for companies that operate in small to midsized communities.

What does turning over your market mean? It means that you can only expect to go so long without interacting in one way or another with the majority of potential buyers in your area. You will either meet with these customers through direct personal interaction or potential customers will hear of your company's actions through other patrons. That interaction will either have a positive effect or a negative effect on future purchases. How it goes is up to you.

If that interaction is in any way negative, your customers will go elsewhere, and you'll have to prospect for new ones.

If your business operates in a small to midsized community, either scenario can be extremely detrimental. Especially if you or your company becomes known for "putting the buck first." It can be detrimental even if your business operates in a large market, with hundreds of thousands or even millions of customers.

With that many customers, it would be hard to personally interact with all buyers or potential buyers. But if the experience for the buyers whom you do interact with is negative, it can still have a tremendous impact on your company. The reason: Customers often find a way to leave their mark of distaste, and often they go beyond bad mouthing you. Now, they use the Internet to do it.

With the Internet, you are not just getting 20 negative impressions because of one unhappy customer, you may be getting 20,000—or more. In many industries, there are web sites with chat rooms for the sole purpose of putting customers' horror stories online for others to view before making a purchase.

For example, Morningstar.com, the web site for the financial rating service, has a chat room. At one point, visitors to the site used that chat room extensively to vent their disfavor with one particular mutual fund offered by Fidelity Investments that was underperforming compared with most in the same category.

Whether the fund was poorly managed as the chat room participants complained it was or merely subject to changing market conditions is a subject of debate. The point here is that fund investors were airing their complaints about both the fund and the company for millions of other investors to see and react to.

Another Internet trick that works well for disgruntled customers is worldwide "slander" e-mail. In this case, customers use e-mail to tell their tale of an atrocious customer service episode, whether true or exaggerated. They distribute it to everyone they can think of, encouraging the recipients to add their own bad experiences and send it on.

Such Internet venting can lead to exponential revenue/profitability losses. It is hard to think how customer service problems could compound in any greater way!

In addition to the Internet, there are other tools unhappy customers can use to voice their anger. They include the Better Business Bureau, the Federal Trade Commission, state and federal consumer protection agencies, and even the attorney general's office in each state.

The moral of the story: Don't believe, for one moment, that you are immune to the feelings of disgruntled customers. Some won't even tell you if they're upset, because they're tired of the type of dealings they've had with many businesses. These are the customers who will quietly go away and then set something in motion that will invariably come back to haunt you or your company.

In this day of the Internet, if you have 2,000 unhappy customers, it means that as many as 40,000 people may know about it. So even if you work in a huge metropolitan area like Los Angeles, New York, or Chicago, if you don't sell well to your customers, the word can spread—in a nanosecond!

You can bet your productivity and profitability will be affected.

And, what if you happen to work in a troubled sector where consumer confidence is low, such as financial services? Try running a company with a reputation of being less-than-honest and throw in a couple of aggressive or less-than-professional salespeople on top of it. That is the perfect recipe for declining profits and increased stress.

Something else to be aware of: A poor sales process can have extremely detrimental effects on both product and service sales. The reason is that even if consumers dislike the salesperson at a particular company, they may still love the product and choose to purchase it again. But, you can bet that they will go elsewhere to buy that product. When it comes to services, however, if consumers dislike the quality of service provided by the salesperson, they will stop using the service regardless of the product. The salesperson, therefore, is closely associated with the product but more so with service.

This is all vitally important when you remember that sales occur in one of three ways: through marketing, referrals, or prospecting to find people to sell to.

Marketing attempts to create the desired image of a product or service, with the goal of enticing the customer to buy (though, as we said earlier most consumers do not trust the adds they see today). Think for a moment about the earlier example of the investment firm Morgan Stanley. The company has been advertising how its financial advisors "embrace the dreams of their clients and make them their own." At the same time, the company has been, allegedly, paying other financial firms to pump up its stocks. The company appears to be saying one thing and doing another. That's the difference between the advertisement or "perceived experience," and the "real experience."

In these instances, the marketing is poorly conceived and relegated to becoming nothing more than the pretty wrapping paper that hides the piece of coal. Unfortunately, in this situation, the consumer never had any chance of knowing about this alleged breech of trust. Quality referrals (which we will look at shortly) create real impressions that can directly speak to the credibility and reliability of a business and those who work for it.

This also relates to creating the authentic experience that we discussed earlier: Remember that the customer is the only one who can pronounce a business authentic. The business itself cannot make this assessment. This authenticity has a dramatic impact on a customer's buying decision. Referrals must be asked for appropriately to preserve this valuable sense of authenticity.

Taking care of people first may take a little bit longer and it may be a little different from most sales approaches, but like anything else great, it's worth the time and effort it requires.

Giving first is not about creating a soft sell; it is about the right way to do things, the right way to treat people. Do what makes people feel good and they will continue to buy from you and to refer others to you who will also continue to buy from you.

Simple common sense dictates that people are naturally programmed to work that way. If you're nice to me, I am more inclined to be nice to you. If you genuinely care about me, I am more inclined to genuinely care about you. The reverse is also true.

Therefore, in the sales process, the referral should come last. We can more effectively generate referrals and those referrals will be more qualified if we first give something to the customer, before we ask them for something in return.

For years, getting that point-of-sale referral has been thought of as a staple of any sales proposition, as one of the first things to do. The moment someone makes a purchase, he or she is most excited about it and will want to share the experience with friends. Since the customer is satisfied at this point, getting that referral will be easier.

Remember, easier is not always better. Yes, you may get that referral early on. But if you do, it does not mean that:

- The customer is happy you asked for it.
- That it is a quality referral.
- That following up on it will be a valuable use of your time or your company's resources.

Receiving a point-of-sale referral does indeed mean that a salesperson has another name and number to call. It just does not mean that the name is worth calling. At least not worth calling any more than randomly picking names from the phone book.

Let us digress for a moment: As we have emphasized many times in this book, there is no way to make your customers trust your salespeople in the first meeting.

The best you can hope to create in that meeting is some kind of a foundation to build on, because building trust with a customer takes time and consistency of action and character.

Let's say you do spend a lot of time trying to genuinely get involved with and understand your customers. Be warned that asking for a point-of-sales referral can send contradictory messages to your customers, and thus, pose a risk to your credibility. This can easily damage any established trust and hinder the further building of those relationships.

Once a customer believes that there are mixed intentions on your part, their guard will go back up. In that case, all of the hard work it took you to get your customer to lower that guard, all of your effort to show that you don't fit into the typical stereotype of the salesperson, will be wasted.

If you're an animal lover, you will understand the following analogy. If not, then keep in mind how instinctual we all are: Think of yourself as a dog that someone sees on the street. The person is a pedestrian who wants to pat your head. The person will first ask your owner, "Is the dog friendly?" Your owner says, "yes."

With caution, the person extends a hand so you, the dog, can sniff it. You wag your tail. You and the person are off to a good start. Then you turn and growl, something the person doesn't expect. The person may jump back and that initial comfort level with you will disappear immediately because the person wonders if you will bite. It will take time for the person to trust you again, if that's even possible.

The same goes for a customer. Changing direction on a customer makes it harder to really get to know them because once someone gets a mixed message from you, they will be careful about dealing with you in the future—if they do so at all. Not only that, your time is valuable; you don't need to spend it rebuilding trust.

As for the quality of referrals, a point-of-sale referral will only be a phone number and permission to use the customer's name, when calling the referral.

Is this the "gold" many salespeople think it is? We don't think so.

If you have just a name and a number, you have to hope that the person you're calling will be swayed enough by the fact that their friend has just made a purchase to listen to you and your presentation. Or, take the time to see you.

But think about this: How much support has been lent to you or to your product by calling on that referral? Not much, because the customer who has given their friend's or family member's name to you has not had a chance to become an advocate of yourself or your business. They just met you or talked with you, and have just made the purchase. Very likely, they can't comfortably or honestly testify to your professionalism, or to that of your company at this early stage.

They may not have had enough time to even tell their friends and family about the purchase, much less rave about you.

Who does that the moment after buying something anyway? People don't make a purchase and then call the world to tell them, "Hi Gary—I just bought this incredible insurance policy—you have to try it." Sorry. That just doesn't happen. Perhaps they will if it's a luxury car or a dream home, but it doesn't mean they're going to tell someone else who needs a fancy car or big house.

Is this the type of empty referral you want? Or, if you manage a company, is this the type of referral you want your salespeople to spend their time getting? Is this smart use of your time? Will this improve productivity?

We think not.

Rather, you'd want a referral because the customer has begun to trust you over time, and has learned to think so highly of you that they feel compelled to tell someone what a good thing they have found.

A solid recommendation sounds like this:

You know Dave, my financial advisor, is unbelievable. You should call him. I checked out at least five financial firms before I found someone who really seemed interested in me, even though I did not have a lot to invest. I've worked with him in good times and bad, and his service has been outstanding. Dave has been calling me every other week during this crazy stock market just to check in and reassure me. He has a daughter in the same school as my daughter. If you are looking for a financial advisor, I would at least give Dave a call first. Or, do you mind if I give him your name and number? He is funny, down to earth, knows his stuff, and really wants to help people build financial security for the future.

Now that's a referral!

If your customer gives you a referral like this, your initial phone call will go well. We can guarantee it and a closed sale will result. It will go well because the person who received your name is anxious to get the same treatment their friend received from you.

When this type of healthy, positive, productive salesperson/customer relationship develops, you may not even have to make that prospect call; your customer's friend or family member may be the one calling you.

That's the way it should work, and we'll bet you have had at least two or three referrals that went this well and felt this good. These referrals really can happen all the time. When a customer feels connected to a salesperson or should we say, when someone feels connected to another person, it is normal to want to spread the good word to those you care about.

Once again: In selling, there is simply nothing more important, and never will be more important, than relationship building. The essence of a personal relationship will simply never be replaced by technology or anything else.

It is true that some companies use technology to automate the majority of customer service issues. For example, Sprint PCS has a talking computer named Clair that really understands what people say quite well. Such devices are meant to control costs and keep people working on the harder customer service issues that require a personal touch.

That said, in sales, the need for personal touches never disappears. You can thank a tradition of a hundred years of poor salesmanship, of snake oil salesmanship, if you will, for that. But that tradition also yields an opportunity for you—to create a unique niche for yourself as a salesperson with true integrity. A real rarity, indeed.

Once you have created that niche for yourself, and you have established sound relationships with your customers, you'll be able to ask for a referral any time without giving it a second thought.

You won't have to wonder, "What did they think of me?" or, "Did I risk the trust of my customer?" You won't have to wonder because you were patient and cared enough to prove yourself to your customer by giving before taking.

Your clients know you are in sales, so how could asking for a referral at this point, and under these positive circumstances, possibly lower a customer's opinion of a salesperson?

In fact, since things have gone so well, chances are, your client will appreciate an opportunity to help you. Giving you the names of people to call will help deepen the bond between the two of you. It gives your customer the chance to give you something back in return. Good people like helping other good people.

Giving salespeople are good people. Keep in mind that it doesn't mean that they have to respond to every customer whim and take all of their time doing so.

Giving can be as simple as just stopping to ask how someone is, waving to them in the street, or sending a note via regular mail. People feel that you're giving to them whenever you make an effort to acknowledge them. That acknowledgment can take a variety of forms.

Whenever someone is nice and caring to another person, people naturally want to reciprocate. Salespeople often fail to remember and utilize this instinct. It's the Golden Rule we all learned as children: Do unto others as you would have others do unto you. Generally, speaking, the basis of the Golden Circle is the Golden Rule. When handled correctly, a customer referral is practicing the precepts of the Golden Rule.

That's why referral is the last of the four steps we've outlined—Prospective Customer Service, World-Class Care, Relationship, and now, Referral. Referral provides the most impact for both the customer and the salesperson/organization at that point.

The Golden Circle is not meant to be the complete sales approach, rather it is meant to be the guidepost to any truly successful, customer-oriented sales system. Any company can tailor it to fit its own culture, its sales style, and its industry. It doesn't matter as long the values we speak of are maintained, and as long as the four steps: Prospective Customer Service, World-Class Care, Relationship, and Referral are practiced and included as the foundation of a corporation's chosen sales system.

The principles of the Golden Circle can be integrated very effectively with many existing sales structures. It does not matter what lead management system a company has. It does not matter what type of follow-up system a company utilizes. It does not matter how aggressive a company's sales goals are. As long as these values and basics are understood and utilized with each and every customer, any company can use the Golden Circle to improve its profits and enhance its own reputation.

The principles of the Golden Circle can be a beacon for you as a salesperson as well. As long as you practice these values and steps with every one of your customers, you will do fine. As long as you form solid, respectful, giving relationships with your customers, you will do fine. And, you and your customer will enjoy doing business. Embrace this approach with the goal of having one constantly moving Golden Circle with each of your clients. You can have 100, 200, or 1,000 circles generating referrals for you every day, if you choose to.

Then, every time you are introduced to a new person via a quality referral, the process begins anew with Prospective Customer Care. And so it will again every time you receive a new referral. The Golden Circle is all about creating continuing, positive, and productive relationships. As long as you practice its principles on a consistent basis, that win-win experience with your customers will have no end.

It is definitely more work doing things this way, some people say it's too much work. However, consistent sales success no matter the economic climate is challenging. Some people like to take short cuts so they will succeed in the short term; this is much easier than succeeding in the long term. Blaming something or someone else rather than taking your share of the responsibility and accountability when the numbers are not hit is also very easy. For that matter, failing out right is easier, than succeeding. But no matter how hard it is, do you really want to be a short-term success or a failure because it is easier?

Chapter 9

How It Began: Ben's Golden Circle Parable

If it doesn't follow the Golden Rule, I don't want to participate in it. We've never made any money bad-mouthing anyone else.

—Morris J. Siegel, director,
Hain Celestial Group, Inc.

Beyond the four rings of the Golden Circle, there are many other things required to make a salesperson successful. There are fundamental truths and activities in selling that no one system will ever be able to replace. This is important to understand because much of what people do not like about selling are the habits you need to develop to put yourself in a situation where you have the opportunity to win. In selling, that comes down to things like prospecting (something everyone knows they need to do but few do enough of), strong organizational skills, excellent time management, determination, creativity, ambition, solid presentation skills, the ability to handle customer concerns quickly and effectively, a thick skin, confidence, and trust in yourself. They are all important and with them you can easily accomplish "good enough" sales results for quite a while. You may even have a few "wow" months.

Seldom though can those results stay on the top for any sustained period of time, especially without taking some sort of toll on other aspects of a salesperson's life. For example, many salespeople who lack the complete and well-rounded approach to sales have to compensate. One way is to work very long hours, the quantity over quality or the "law of averages approach" as we like to call it. These work habits can have a detrimental affect on a person's family life. This person does not spend as much time as he possibly could have with his significant other or children. He misses special events and the little things that he may not get the chance to see or do again, which over time will create an emotional imbalance and then spill back into his work life. Or if this person is single and has the extra time to spare on work, many times, she will start to eat poorly, skip exercising, and stop paying close attention to her own health. Again this will end up having an effect on performance at work. And finally if the other two areas are doing okay, a person still needs time for him- or herself, time to do things unrelated to work and enjoy a fuller life, maybe it is a walk with your dog, a day at the beech, a skiing trip, a work out, or maybe just time to sleep in a hammock in the backyard. If you do not do these things, there can be a negative effect on your work life. You can only run so long and so far at "optimal speed" if you are running out of gas or if everything is not working properly.

Being a salesperson is hard work. You have to deal with rejection, constant repetition, inconsistent income, pressure to hit sales goals, and tremendous competition for the same business. So in order to consistently perform at your best and to last, it is important that you keep everything in balance:

- Do all the things a salesperson needs to do day-to-day to keep presenting yourself with opportunities to sell to people.
- Sell using the principles of the Golden Circle.

- Never work too much so that you disregard your family, your health, and your own peace of mind.

Everything needs to be balanced so you can keep a clear and relaxed mind and so your body will always get you from point a to point b, without undue trouble. Believe it or not, everything is more connected than you realize. Doing everything possible for career success seldom brings the happiness. Be happy first, then the success will come.

So where did this all come from, what got it started? It came from a page in Ben's life—from a difficult job that taught him some profound, life-altering lessons that have shaped his career as a salesperson—lessons he'd like to share. Here is Ben's story:

About 13 years ago, I lost my job as a fitness instructor and part time salesperson at Saco Sport & Fitness, a health club in Saco, Maine. I lost my job because an arsonist set the club on fire and destroyed it.

Since the fitness industry in Maine was very small at the time, I couldn't find another comparable job. So, I decided to take an odd job until the club reopened. Reopening took a full year. In that time, I worked for a good friend who owned a sea urchin shipping business. The urchins where caught and packed in Maine, brought down to Boston, and then sent to Japan for use in restaurants. It was actually quite a good business—for the owner, at least.

This was my role: six to seven days a week, between 3 P.M. and 5 P.M., I would go down to the docks in Kennebunkport with a truck to wait for the urchin divers to return with their catch. Next, I would carry and load all of the "totes" (boxes that hold about 70 pounds of fish) onto the truck and drive back to the plant where the packing process took place.

The plant was in the back of an unheated, corner store in nearby Kennebunk. It was one big open room with two big racks made of plywood and PVC pipe that were tilted at a slight, downward angle, with just enough space between each pipe so that the urchins could be separated from the seaweed and the rocks.

When we got back from the dock with the urchins, we would bring the smelly, wet, 70-pound totes into the plant and, one by one, empty them onto the racks. Then we would roll the urchins to the end of the rack into an insulated cardboard box that sat on a big fish scale. We would weigh each box, seal it, and then lug them one by one to the back of a 35-foot cooler. After that, we would pull all of the nasty little urchin spikes out of our cold wet fingers, dump the water out of our gloves, and go back to do it all over again. All the while, the only thing we had to keep our minds off this awful job in that shack-of-a-plant was a small transistor radio.

To say it was hard, trying work is an understatement. We'd be working in the unheated back of that store during the long, cold, Maine winter. By 9 P.M., each night, we'd still have about 25 totes to unload and pack. So we would trudge out through the snow to the truck in our wet boots for another 70-pound tote, bring it in, and put it on the rack for sorting and packing. And so on and so forth until about 1 A.M. Even though each time we went through this routine we thought we might be able to get things done quicker, something always happened to keep us there until 1.

I remember each night when I finally got home to bed, I would be thinking about how much "fun" it would be to get up at 5 A.M. to go load up the truck with the 50- to 60-pound insulated cardboard boxes full of urchins, by myself, no less. (Obviously, it was not fun.) I would then drive the truck one hour and forty-five minutes to the Boston airport terminal, unload it, and drive back to Maine. At that point, I'd either sleep for another hour or just drink coffee and then go back to the dock at 3 P.M. for another run at it.

Now all the while I was doing this I worked with two very interesting gentlemen, we'll call them Sean and John (not their real names, of course). Sean stood about 6'3", and sported long black hair, a bushy black beard, and wore clothes right out of the Beverly Hillbillies. John was about 6'4" and had a huge frame. He had the same black beard and bushy hair, but he wore eyeglasses that darkened in the sunlight, so I couldn't look him in the eye. I remember clearly the first time I met John. He was walking out of the woods wearing a bright orange hunter's vest and carrying a rifle. If it weren't for the fact that it was deer-hunting season, and

*my close friend, Peter (who owned the business), reas-
suring me that John was not going to kill me, I'd say
John looked like my worst nightmare.*

*Needless to say, we didn't meet down at the coun-
try club. Now if you add working with these two guys to
9 or 10 hours of lugging around cold, smelly sea
urchins, in a very cold and wet place—you've got one
great working environment!*

*I had been working at this wonderful job for three
months. I no longer washed my jeans when I got home
because I was too tired. So I would just come in, throw
them on the radiator, kiss my fiancé goodnight, and
fall asleep. I woke up at dawn, put on my now rock-
hard (but warm) jeans, and go back to work. If you can
imagine, the smell. . . .*

*Anyway, at this point, I realized this job was not
fun. Especially for $7 an hour and no benefits. But
what could I do? My passion was to work in the fitness
industry again. Plus I was trying to save money for my
wedding, which was coming up in seven months. So, I
decided to stick it out until the club opened again.
Which I prayed would be soon.*

*A few more days went by and I figured that I
should try to make the best of it. So finally Sean, John,
and I started to joke around a little bit and get to know
one another.*

*Sean and John would make fun of the fact that I
was a salesperson and that I must have thought I was
pretty smart and smooth. I learned that Sean kept*

about six cars in his front yard that didn't work, and he liked to work on them when he could, in hopes of getting one to work (people do that in Maine—broken down cars are like lawn decorations). So needless to say, I had plenty of material on him. I would poke fun at John (when John did not have a rifle) because he picked up scrap metal in his spare time and dropped it off at a recycling plant for extra cash. I had plenty of material to work with about John as well.

As time went on though, we all learned more about each other. Sean was a mechanic at heart, John drove around picking up scrap metal, and I was a salesperson. We all agreed that being a salesperson must be the worst job. But, as I spent more and more time with these guys, I learned that Sean took a lot of pride in fixing those cars in his yard. He was good at it, and when he finally got one of these pieces of trash to run, he drove it around to show all his friends and explain exactly what it took to get it to work. And, occasionally, he even sold one of them. That was a big deal to Sean. Was I interested in that? Not at first. But when I started listening, I began to understand more about Sean and just how much it meant to him.

John liked to drive his truck around every morning picking up scrap metal because he could be his own boss and make his own hours. He could do his job while he had his coffee in the morning and listened to his favorite radio station. When I really started listening to him, I realized he really appreciated his freedom

*and job security, plus he was paying his bills. I also
began to realize that he was only working with us packing sea urchins so he could get the extra money that he
needed to buy his wife the engagement ring she never
had. He wanted to surprise her with one on their an-
niversary. That really showed me what kind of guy
John was. He was a great guy, with a huge heart who
loved his wife very much.*

*As I grew to be more open and comfortable with
Sean and John, we started having more fun. I actually
started to look forward to going to this miserable job
just so I could see these guys again and goof around.
Believe me, it is hard to look forward to a job like this.
But if you spend all night thinking of another broken-
down-car-in-the-front-yard joke, sometimes you just
can't wait to use it.*

*From this experience with sea urchins and Sean and
John, I had an epiphany that changed me forever: I had
just spent three lousy months dreading going to work,
not enjoying myself at all, doing it all for very little
money, and feeling sorry for myself. So I asked myself,
why didn't I just take the time to get to know these two
guys right from the beginning? What was I thinking?*

*I could have made this situation a lot better, a lot
quicker than I did.*

*After thinking about it, I really had no answer.
That is except for the one I really did not want to face
and it was this: I did not care to take the time to get to*

know them because of how I assumed they would be. That was a mistake, and that is why I finally "got it." Now I think of my job packing sea urchins as one the most important experiences of my life.

I started to realize that soon I would be working for the health club again because it was scheduled to open in another four months. This made me think about my job. I was looking forward to getting back to work—without sea urchins—to getting back to selling—in a heated building—and making okay money for a living. That was a nice thought because with more money, I could buy more food and that was reassuring.

That's when I started to think very carefully about selling.

I thought about how I had been trained to sell. I remember the manipulative things like "if I could, would you?" Or, "so your husband makes all the decisions in the family" when speaking to women who wanted to consult their husbands before making a purchase. I thought of all of the standard sales training techniques that where popular then and are still popular now.

I realized that all of those things were just not right, down right foolish really, because they have little to do with getting someone to buy from you. Instead, I began to think how important it was to get to know people, how I had discovered so much about Sean and John once I took an interest in them. Once I got to know them, and found out what was really important to them, I began to value those things, and the same thing happened to them as they began to learn about me.

I related that to selling—if you want to know what works, take the time to get to know who people are and let them get to know who you are.

You don't need lines, or tricks, or psychology. You need to genuinely care about people and show it. They, in turn, will begin to care about you. They will prefer to buy from you, they will want their friends to buy from you, and you will want to see them happy and satisfied.

I was energized! I knew that all the fluff didn't matter, so I swore never to use those silly sales tricks again!

The club reopened, and I went back to work. I told my boss that I was going to win the Salesperson of the Year Award for the worldwide fitness industry, an honor that is bestowed each year on one individual by the International Health Racquet and Sports Club Association, a trade group in the fitness field that represents more than 6,000 clubs worldwide.

It was the highest award in sales that I could achieve, and I was determined to win it by getting to know my customers.

I went back to selling memberships, and in the process, made it my top priority to learn about every single person I was selling to. Not just what they wanted (like a needs analysis) but, rather, who they were because that's what I cared about.

The results surprised me. I sold so much more than I ever had before and I had smiling customers all along the way. But more important than that, by the end of the year I had so many more friends than I did when I started. I felt like the luckiest guy in town because I knew everyone, liked everyone, and they seemed to like me. I had made real connections with the people around me and it felt right.

And, yes, I won the award.

Ben created a positive world for himself, as you can with the Golden Circle. Follow its precepts and you will create a very upbeat, energizing environment for yourself—something that is usually very hard to find in the world of sales.

You will change the whole feel of working in or for a sales-based organization—the balance will shift from the grind of constant repetition and rejection, to lots of casual—but productive fun—and many meaningful relationships. Sales will become an exhilarating job. More topnotch salespeople will want to work with you and for your company, when they learn of what you do and "catch the fever."

Is this realistic, you may be wondering? Absolutely. Salespeople should feel that they are surrounded by, and work with, lots of friends who also happen to be their clients. Ask yourself this: If you worked in, or could create an environment like this for others to work in, can you imagine anyone wanting to work somewhere else once they have experienced it? No way!

As human resources experts will testify, millions of people in this country will stay in jobs simply because they enjoy them and not because of the salary. The reverse is also true; people will leave well-paying jobs because they believe that they will be happier somewhere else. Pay is important to most people—but only if they are happy and enjoy their work.

Knowing that employee turnover is an extremely expensive issue for most sales organizations, an employer would be wise to help their salespeople feel good about what they do as well as help them to produce and pay them well. The Golden Circle can help provide precious job satisfaction.

Another thing to note: It is true that the concept of the Golden Circle stems from nothing more than common sense. Still, the principles of the Golden Circle cannot be correctly and effectively utilized unless two other things support them. They are:

1. An organization that looks on these values as a real and essential part of its mission, and properly and consistently trains its employees on how to use them.
2. A sales management team that internalizes and emulates all of these values and fundamentals, and uses them as the foundation of the company's sales program.

If you do not carry the values of the customer through to the training process and management process, you cannot expect this system to yield its best results.

Just as customers know how they want to be treated, so do employees. You have to train them with materials that stress the value of a relationship, that stress ethical sales practices and ethical treatment of customers. You must also manage your sales staff with those same ethics. You must give your employees the direction they need to succeed and you must work just as hard at building relationships with your employees, as you do with your customers. Don't try to find a short cut there.

Ignore these requirements, and the values of the customer will have no chance of penetrating throughout the business. Ignore these requirements, and you will prevent the organization from consistently delivering those values back to the customers and in the process, you will fail to consistently hit your sales targets.

YOU WILL BREAK THE GOLDEN CIRCLE

You might think of the Golden Circle of Business as the Rubric's cube of sales, sales training, and sales management. The concept can be easy enough to master. If everyone in your organization shares the same values, then you will have all the right colors on all the right sides of the cube. Things will go quite smoothly.

However, if individuals in your company have different values, then you will have mixed colors on all sides of the cube and it will be extremely difficult to get everyone aligned. You will find there is miscommunication because people don't understand one another. Things will go awry, and no one will be happy about it. Take your pick: Things can be simple or very complicated. Which way would you prefer?

It is true that human nature dictates that people will often fail to grasp the ease of simple ideas. They'll do things the hard way, over and over until they discover that there is another, better way of doing things. The good news is that things really don't have to be that hard in the first place. Once you know that, once you really understand that, it's a relief that life can be quite simple and enjoyable. You will be able to create it, if you internalize the values of the Golden Circle.

The Golden Circle is about bringing those values to your customers each and every day, while you conduct business with them. It's about aligning yourself and your business to those values over the long term.

One of the keys to creating success in business and in life is to focus on one thing at a time, to learn it well, then to move on to something else. So, build Prospective Customer Service, World-Class Care, Relationship, and Referral into your foundation and build your house from there. Keep simple things simple and do things one at a time. Remember Picasso once remarked that he spent most of his adult life trying to forget his formal training. The same is true in selling effectively. It's not all the "advanced sales techniques" that closes more sales; it is focusing on the simplicity of what you are doing. We conclude this book by talking in depth about those values.

Chapter 10

Dale's Golden Circle "Words to Live By"

No amount of ability is of the slightest avail without honor.

—Andrew Carnegie (1835–1919)

Now, we return to, and reemphasize, the values that a great salesperson and a great business need to hold dear. Please think about them carefully. If you only take one thing from this book, let it be that you realize the profound importance of values. In this chapter, Dale explores the values we both hold most dear.

Integrity: The state of being whole, honest, upright, sincere, with uncompromising adherence to moral and ethical principles (*Webster's Dictionary*, Eleventh Edition).

We tend to assume that a person has integrity until they do something that demonstrates that they don't. Once integrity is compromised, it is extremely difficult to regain. Compromised integrity is like an avalanche; it gains momentum as it tumbles faster and faster, destroying all before it and the foundation of trust that you worked so hard to build.

Success magazine founder Dr. Orison Swett Marden once posed the notion about the trust that we have in our world, how we take it for granted, and what it would be like to be without it:

Suppose we lived in a world where natural things would lie and deceive us as a man would; a world where the mountains, the sea, the forests, and the rivers were all shams; where the earth looks rich and fruitful, would mock us by refusing harvest in return for our seed; where what appears like a beautiful landscape would prove only a deceptive mirage; where gravitation could not be depended upon; where the planets would not keep in their orbits; where the atoms were not true to the laws within them. (Lexington, KY: Successful Achievement, 1971, Successful Achievement, Vol. 2, pp. 753–754)

How could we exist in such a world? There is no substitute for truthfulness and honesty; they are the foundation on which your career will be built, and your work will be judged. Many a politician has assumed that a few less-than-truthful statements would be quickly for-gotten—and paid a high price for making that assump-tion. You do not want to be known in your career or business as someone who believes that *truth is but a lie undiscovered.*

As you go forward in your career, the book of business that you develop must be built on the solid foundation of truth and honesty. You always want to be regarded as a person who can be trusted to deliver what you promise, a person of unquestionable integrity. It will be a corner-stone that will bear the weight of all your dealings with customers in the future. It will continually bring you a great number of referrals from past customers who value you as a person who keeps a promise.

If you are ever tempted to be less than truthful in your dealings with others, remember the following: Without truth, your career will be a constant process of rebuilding relationships. You will not enjoy the fruits of an endless supply of referrals, because your relationships have not been built on the foundation of integrity that your customers and coworkers deserve.

> **Determination:** The quality of being resolute with firmness of purpose. (*Webster's Dictionary*, Eleventh Edition)

The foundation for a career is built from many bricks. Determination is one of those bricks that can be easily misplaced by a need to take short cuts to success. Some of us have the luxury of being granted shortcuts, whether it is wealth or connections. Still, if you understand that hard work must be the basis of your craft, if you master the tools necessary for your success, you will have a stable base from which you can build your book of business, and you will never feel the need to rely on shortcuts.

There will be times when your determination will be tested and your resolve will weaken. When you wonder, "Is this really worth all of the effort I am putting into it?" When those times come, and they will, you must look inward and make that judgment for yourself.

A couple by the name of Jeneen and Tim Hamilton have been faced with that question many times. Just over two years ago, Janeen found out that she was pregnant and, like most all couples finding out that they where going to be parents, they where thrilled. However, this normally enchanting time turned out to be the biggest test of their lives.

On the day Jeneen went in for her first ultrasound, everything went great, she heard the little heartbeat, and it was quite an experience. When it came time for the second ultrasound, Tim joined her so that they could both experience this wonderful event (if you're a parent I am sure that you remember), but this one did not go quite as well. There was no heartbeat to be heard. They were rushed to the hospital to save the baby. When they arrived at the ER, the doctor immediately checked again with another ultrasound and the heartbeat was there. But there was also something else.

They discovered a spot on the back of the baby's head. A specialist looked at the spot in case there was anything that they needed to be concerned about. After the specialist reviewed all the tests, he informed Janeen and Tim that he thought their little girl had a genetic disorder that causes dramatic deformation, and that either during or soon after birth the baby would die. To conduct further tests, the doctors instructed Jeneen to have an amniocentesis.

Tim asked the doctor if they had ever been wrong about these ultrasounds and the doctor said never and that he would bet his paycheck that this diagnosis was correct. When the amniocentesis results came back, they showed that the diagnosis was in fact not correct, however, there were other problems. The baby was what is known as a "frozen baby," meaning that it was trapped in an area where it could not move, this caused organs to be underdeveloped and for limbs and joints to be misaligned. The doctors encouraged them to abort the baby because she would undoubtedly die at birth, but they would not. Tim and Jeneen agreed that they would see this through, even if only to kiss their daughter before she died. Jeneen continued to carry their daughter, and the baby continued to grow but could not move. And, at 25 weeks, Jeneen went into labor.

After being in the delivery room for a while (and dilating to 2 centimeters), the nurse came in and removed the heart rate monitor that monitored the baby's heartbeat. When the parents asked why, the nurse informed them that they were there to save the mother and not the baby. Although in labor, Jeneen got up and left that hospital with her husband; they were not going to stay in any hospital that was not going to try to save their daughter.

They went home and for 13 more weeks Jeneen stayed at home, with her feet up, so that the baby could develop more and have a better chance of surviving. Jeneen made it to 38 weeks, almost to term, and then they went in to the hospital to have their daughter for a scheduled c-section. In the delivery room, they planned to have their baby baptized immediately after she was born and made all the arrangements (because they did not expect her to survive). As the doctors brought their daughter into this world, Jeneen said to her husband, "let her die in your arms, make sure that she dies in your arms." Then, something happened that was not supposed to, the baby cried. Unbelievably, the baby made it and they named their daughter Faith.

Since Faith's birth, it has not been an easy road for the three of them. Since Faith had blockages in her throat, she required a tracheotomy and needed to be on a ventilator 24 hours a day. She has been through 13 surgeries, gone into cardiac arrest and flat lined, been through pneumonia, and has more surgeries to come. She also has lived at the hospital for the past 17 months.

Faith lived when they said she would die and Faith stands on her own two feet when they said she would never stand. All of the nurses at the hospital say that Faith is the happiest little girl that they know and that she loves to have fun. Tim works harder than he ever has to support the family and they are both constantly back and forth to the hospital to spend time with Faith. Her parents have taught her sign language and they are hoping that sometime soon, they will be able to take her home. Has it been easy on the whole family, no way. Do they keep going and continue to try harder every day, of course they do. They are happiest together and because of their determination, they will always be a family.

Many people may say that this story has nothing to with business; I think it has everything to do with business. Your level of determination is predicated on how much you value the outcome and purpose of what you are working towards. I can think of nothing more important than fighting for life of your child, in business, if you can not find an intense level of passion and desire to achieve your purpose or an inherent need to accomplish what you have set out to do (well beyond because you have to) then you will have a very hard time achieving any level of great accomplishments that may lie ahead of you. If you have no passion or need to do the work you do, then you may be better of finding something else to work toward.

Even then, you will still have failures and you will have successes during your career. Challenges will be plenty and how you handle these challenges will determine how long you will stay the course. The secret to keeping going whether it is for your family or your business is your determination to succeed.

The American writer IK Marvel (1822–1908) wrote:

We have briefly reviewed being determined, doing the hard work necessary to master your craft. There is no substitute to the resolute determination that is necessary for you to forge this critical foundation piece. You will be amazed at what you will accomplish once you are convinced that you will devote the time, energy and determination to realize your dreams and desires. Resolve is what makes a person manifest; not puny resolve, not crude determinations, not errant purpose but that strong and indefatigable will, which treads down difficulties and danger, which kindles the eye and brain with the proud pulse beat toward the unattainable. Will makes all persons giants.

Competence: Having suitable or sufficient skill, knowledge, and experience; properly qualified. (*Webster's Dictionary*, Eleventh Edition)

The enthusiasm that a person has when he or she enters a new field of endeavor can quickly turn to discouragement if that person does not become competent at their craft quickly. However, a novice must realize that anyone who is new rarely possesses the competencies needed to do a job consistently well, and it will take time to attain competence. It is not to say that people are not capable of learning, but your success will largely depend on who is there to assist you on the road to mastery.

Mastering your craft, no matter what it is, will require effort, determination, and a willingness to listen and learn from your mentor. I remember my first job as a strawberry-picker when I was in the seventh grade. I thought picking strawberries would be such an easy job.

You're out in the field, in the sun with lots of strawberries to eat—and you get paid for it.

Needless to say, reality came very quickly. Yes, I could pick fast and eat just as fast, but I was incompetent. The berries that I picked were bruised, and, as a result, every one of the boxes that I picked was rejected as unsuitable for the stand.

This was such a simple job, so how could I possibly have screwed it up? After all, they were only strawberries. I lasted for less than two hours on my first real job. I hadn't paid attention to the instructions. I did it my way, instead. I had forgotten, that, without a quality product, I could not be in the strawberry-picking business.

But the next year I went back. This time, I listened to what the foreman said and did things her way. This time, I lasted the entire picking season and, at the end, earned a cash bonus and six extra boxes of strawberries to take home.

What made the difference? It was my attitude, and my openness and willingness to learn from the person who was experienced. Following instructions did not stifle my creativity or subjugate my spirit. Rather, it made my job easier and more productive. I became competent as a strawberry-picker and got a bonus for work well done.

The price we pay for failure to master our craft is far greater than the time and effort expended to master it well in the first place and reap the rewards.

The greatest real estate trainer and mentor in my opinion is Floyd Wickman, creator of the "Sweathogs" real estate training program, the most well-known training program in the industry. He constantly reminded all who took his Sweathog Training that, "Education without application, is worse than worthless." Floyd insisted that his students become competent, confident, and natural at what they do, so they would be prepared to handle any situation with professionalism and a high level of skill.

Because of the things I learned from Floyd as a trainer and as a friend, I always remember to tell all whom I teach: Pay the price, master your craft, listen to those who know and become a person whom others seek out because of the your competence.

Loyalty: The state of being loyal; a feeling of faith or allegiance. (*Webster's Dictionary,* Eleventh Edition)

Loyalty is not blind. It is much more than simply following orders. Loyalty can only be earned through deeds and actions that are just and consistent. If you want to earn loyalty from the people you hire, from the people you work for, or from those with whom you have business relationships, you must earn it through your actions and deeds. It is imperative that you display the loyalty to your company, to your partner, to your customers, and to your loved ones. False loyalty does nothing but undermine the foundation of the enterprise to which you have committed yourself.

George Washington, in his inaugural address said:

The foundations of our national policy will be laid in the pure and immutable principles of private morality; and the preeminence of free government be exemplified by the attributes which can win the affections of its citizens, and command the respect of the world. I dwell on this prospect with every satisfaction which an ardent love for my country can aspire; since there is no truth more thoroughly established, than that there exists in the economy and course of nature, an indissoluble union between virtue and happiness, between duty and advantage, between the genuine maxims of an honest and magnanimous policy and the solid rewards of public prosperity and felicity. . . .

Washington's entire life was an example of love of country, of fellow man, and of God. The loyalty that he displayed to the cause of freedom, even in its darkest hour, has made the father of our country such an example that the word "loyalty" is forever associated with his name.

There are going to be times that you may want to criticize those for whom you work. If you must judge them, make sure that your judgment is just, and that both sides of the story are known and understood.

Also remember that loyalty is a two-way street. It is not only important for employees to be loyal to the company, those who are responsible for management have an obligation to be morally and ethically loyal to their employees.

Recently, we have heard many stories about top managers of large companies saying one thing to their employees, and privately doing something completely the opposite. It is not surprising that these incidents have had an incredible effect on the loyalty that employees feel for their companies. No doubt, many employees would like to feel loyalty, but how can they when they've been deceived?

Loyalty implies unswerving allegiance to someone or something for consistently honest and good behavior.

Be loyal to those in your life who have earned it. Be loyal to yourself and those whom you love. In the end, there is nothing stronger than the bond that is forged by your commitment and loyalty to those who have put their trust in you.

Cooperation: The action of working or acting together for a common purpose or benefit. (*Webster's Dictionary,* Eleventh Edition)

The snow was swirling around a car that had slid into the ditch. The young driver was in tears and explaining that she had to get to her job and had no money to get towed out. Each driver who passed her stopped to lend a hand until one became six. The seventh was the driver of a 4 × 4 pickup truck. The six could not budge the car; it had so deeply sunk into the snow as she had tried to back out. But, the driver of the pickup had a tow rope that was quickly fastened to the car. With the help of the crew of seven Good Samaritans and the truck, the car could now be pulled out with ease.

This is the kind of cooperation that can happen every day. Each of us has had a friend who has stood by us in our hour of deepest despair and kept us from giving up. That friend has helped us turn defeat into a new beginning.

In the corporate world, we hear often about company "teams" that work together to accomplish much. This word is overused and abused. In reality, the structure that many companies have is no more than that of a landlord and a serf. If, you do not do what the "team" or management wants, you will be banished from your land. Is that any way to build a team? I think not.

I would be much more inclined to use the word, "partnership" instead of team. The most successful companies see each employee as a vital part of the customer relationship cycle. For example, the person who answers the phone in a friendly and courteous manner is far more important than most companies realize. Yes, they say it is important, but when it comes to rewarding that person for providing the first bridge to potential lifetime customer relationships, all is forgotten. They may place much more importance on a CEO who has lost employee trust and respect. Then they reward that CEO with a Golden Parachute for failure and incompetence.

The cooperation of all is vital for the success of the enterprise. If companies truly want to succeed for the long term, they must discard the old concept that the people at the top must make the most money. If, you really want a team concept to work, then look to a successful sports team. It is not the manager who is paid the most. It is the outstanding players that make the team a team. They have a special way of magnifying the accomplishments of the team. The cooperation of each player is critical. The players know that cooperation of each team member is the key to success.

The greatest injustice is to reward equals unequally or unequals equally. If you have the best receptionist in the business, he or she is worth a great deal. As the initial point of contact, the receptionist enables each member of the partnership to help the others by providing a solid bridge.

If you want to really have partnership with your employees, come down to earth and listen to your employees with your heart. Forget about the "company survey," people tend to answer them feeling that any unsatisfactory answers will have consequences. If you want to have cooperation as one of the foundations for your company's success—you must first give it.

At the other end of the spectrum, beware of the board of directors that rubber stamps all decisions, collects a check, and pats itself on the back for a job well done. It is not acting responsibly. Cooperation is not about agreeing on everything or surrendering; it is a responsible way of ensuring that the common purpose is achieved for the common good.

> **Leadership:** The ability to provide guidance and direction, with decisiveness and inspiration. (*Webster's Dictionary,* Eleventh Edition)

The world looks for leaders, it looks for women and men who are willing to take on the responsibility, challenges, and the trust that is vested in them. People want good leaders, and there are no two ways around that. They want to know that there is legitimacy in the person who is leading them—legitimacy of character, judgment, common sense, and concern for those they lead.

The past several years have exposed the leaders of some companies for what they really are: greedy, selfish, and mean-spirited individuals who conveyed their sincerity in a manner that has mocked the very words they used.

Ben Franklin said, "Money never made a man happy yet; there is nothing in its nature to produce happiness. It's a fact of human nature: The more money a person has, the more the person wants. Instead of filling a vacuum, money makes one. A great bank account can never make a person rich. It is the mind that makes the body rich. No person is rich, however much money or land they may possess, who has a poor heart. We are rich or poor according to what we are, not according to what we have."

Above all, a leader must possess integrity. It is not to say that a leader cannot be wealthy, but he or she must possess integrity to be truly respected. So often, the failure of once successful companies has had more to do with the character of the leader than with the current market changes or trends. Because of that lack of character, once the trust of any leader has been compromised, it doesn't matter what directives, plans, or objectives are established; the people he once led will have lost their faith and the spark of enthusiasm, energy, and creative power they once had, will have died. Conversely, a true leader inspires those who he or she leads. The respect, pride, and happiness that a true leader brings to the enterprise are what unite the company and the employee.

In the words of Robert Waters, "There is no success without honor; no happiness without a clear conscience; no use in living at all if only for one's self. It is not at all necessary for you to make a fortune, but it is necessary, absolutely necessary, that you should become a fair-dealing, honorable, useful person, radiating goodness and cheerfulness wherever you go, and making your life a blessing."

Consistency: Steadfast adherence to the same principles, course of action, or form. (*Webster's Dictionary,* Eleventh Edition)

The quality of our work and the depth of the business relationships that we value will be measured by the consistency with which we deliver the service we promised. It has been said that the quality of our work will have a great deal to do with the quality of our life. The quality of our work will be judged by the manner in which we consistently provide world-class care for those relationships we have built through the years.

In a company, there is nothing more debilitating than inconsistent leadership. Granted, the cause must be honorable and the work valuable to your clients, but the leadership of a company must have a consistency that is backed by actions and deeds, and not just words. It does not take long for the average person to discover that, what is expected of them is not expected of those in leadership positions. For a leader, the consistency and quality of leadership will be a measure of that leader's success. People put their trust and faith in a leader based on that consistency.

In a similar vein, the consistency and quality of the service or product that you deliver to your customers will be the measure of your success. Still, every one of us has, at one time or another, made a conscious decision to do what we considered was "good enough," but the customer didn't see it that way. In truth, the shortcuts we took only resulted in delivering something that was not up to the standards that we had previously set for ourselves—and we knew it.

What can you say to the person who received the inconsistent product or service? Not much can be said, actually. Your actions have spoken for themselves loudly and clearly. If, you are ever tempted to deliver less than your best, don't do it. All of your hard work and your reputation are at stake.

Consistency in what you do is the glue that holds your success together. It will result in repeat business and referrals because the customer knows that the service or product will be of the highest quality delivered in a consistent manner.

No matter how trivial the task, how minor the assignment, how inconsequential the job, it is your consistent performance that matters. Always deliver the best product and service possible in the same consistent manner to all. The payoff will come in repeat business and referrals, as well as the pride in a job well done.

Persistence: The ability to continue steadily or firmly in some state, purpose or course of action, or to endure tenaciously. (*Webster's Dictionary,* Eleventh Edition)

The success stories that we revere are simply the legends of inventors, scientists, explorers, and writers who refused to quit regardless of how long it took to achieve their vision. In your own life, I'm sure you can think of a time when you wanted something so badly that you would do what it took, almost anything to achieve your goal. Each of us has faced a challenge that we thought was impossible to complete. Yet, we found a way to complete the task, and to do it well.

Achieving any goal involves taking three steps forward and two steps back. It is perseverance that keeps you on track. There is no mystery as to how great rivers were formed; it was the slow process of erosion that wore down the hardest stone. Likewise, in your career and in your life, you will have many obstacles to overcome and in time you will overcome them all. It will only be a matter of determining what you really want, and the only one who can stop you is yourself.

There was a woman who dreamed about earning her doctorate degree but she faced innumerable obstacles. She was often tempted to quit for many reasons, personal, financial, and just not believing she could complete it. She was under enormous stress. She took out student loans, worked a full-time job, took care of the family and the dog, and did all the housework while she was writing her dissertation. The amount of energy and determination she needed to accomplish this goal was incredible. Long days, longer nights, yet she persisted, did immeasurable amounts of research and wrote one page a day on her dissertation. Her dissertation was 360-pages long and she finished one year from the time she started.

The completed dissertation was submitted to her doctoral committee and after a few minor changes, it was unanimously accepted and she graduated with honors. Today, she is working at a university and is the director of a program to assist low-income students to get their college degrees. The persistence that she showed to reach her goal was remarkable.

How do I know that this happened? The woman I have told you about is Nicole, my daughter.

Never let anything stand in the way of your vision whether it is an educational goal, a job-related goal, a family-related goal, or a personal achievement that you have always wanted to do, just keep going until you get it. It is amazing what someone can endure on their way to achieving an important goal, as long as they continue to persevere. And, surprisingly enough when you finally reach your goal, all of the effort you put in won't seem quite as hard.

Love: Affectionate concern for the well being of others. (*Webster's Dictionary,* Eleventh Edition)

Love is the foundation of everything that is good and worthwhile. Every human being, every creature on this earth, whether it can express it or not has this undeniable requirement to love and be loved. Without love, your life is unfinished, the circle is not closed, and remains open searching for the last link that will complete it. Too many people pretend not to need love, but they only hide a greater need for it.

As a child, the love you received from your mother and father was not one of conditions but given from the heart and everlasting. While our parents may not like some of the things we do as children and adolescents, the bond of love is not broken.

There are times in life when we feel defeated and alone with nowhere to go. But there is always a light, and it can come in strange ways. Remember, "A misty morning does not signify a cloudy day," says an ancient proverb.

The memories that we forge through the years are of times together that bring a flood of warm and wonderful memories. Do not let your job be a reason to miss these precious times. Always remember that the job will be gone some day. When it is, will you have the memories of the important times with your family and all who love you to sustain you in your search for another job? Remember, it is only a job.

Love has a habit of coming in strange ways to each of us. Sometimes it is there and we don't recognize it. Sometimes it is hidden in an action that we need to reconsider to discover. Sometimes we only catch a glimpse of it around the holidays. Most often, however, it is right in front of us with no conditions, and no strings. Just love, pure and simple, waiting to come into our hearts and enrich our lives by being what it is.

Love is the golden bond that binds us to our families and loved ones. We live our lives with truth and honor for them, and for ourselves.

As an old Russian proverb states, "Love is a ring, and a ring has no end." So it is true with the Golden Circle. We wish you the most and brightest success in your future.

References

"Investor Confidence Survey." *Accounting Today*, Vol. 18 (2004), p. 10.

Marden, O. S. *Successful Achievement*, Vol 2. (Lexington, KY: Successful Achievement, 1971), pp. 753–754.

Mathews and Wacker. "The Dance of Authenticity" (pp. 105–107). In *Business: The Ultimate Resource*. ed. D. Goleman (New York: Purseus, 2002).

Mitchell, D. G. "American IK Marvel," In *Successful Achievement*, Vol 1 (Lexington, KY: Successful Achievement, 1971), p. 193.

Moeller, L. H., Mathews, S. K., and Rothenberg, R. "The Better Half: The Artful Science of ROI Marketing, Strategy & Composition." *Strategy & Business* (Spring 2003), 32–45.

Rigby, D., Reichfeld, F. F., and Schefer, P. "Avoid the Perils of CRM." *Harvard Business Review*, vol. 80, no. 2 (2002), pp. 101–109.

Schultz, H. 24-Hour Fitness Convention, San Diego, CA, March 23, 2002.

Waters, R. *Successful Achievement*, Vol. 1 (Lexington, KY: Successful Achievement, 1971), p. 1314.

About the Authors

DALE MIDGLEY

With more than 30 years of experience in Real Estate, Dale's career has spanned everything from sales associate, manager, broker owner, research consultant, management consultant, college teacher, and conference/rally speaker. He started in real estate in 1967—when the sale of his first listing netted him $0.00 dollars, he has come a long way since then.

He has been the director of sales and management development for a major real estate franchise and a certified trainer for Floyd Wickman Associates. Dale has taught Prelicense, Sales Associate, Broker/Owner-Manager Seminars regionally, nationally, and internationally.

Dale was most recently the director of sales and management for Weichert Real Estate Affiliates, Morris Plains, New Jersey. Weichert Realtors was founded in 1969 and is the largest independently owned real estate company in the United States, with annual sales of over $52 billion. Dale is also extremely active as a convention, conference, and seminar speaker delivering more than 100 presentations a year.

Dale has that rare ability to make the complex simple and the familiar new. Combine that with good old Maine common sense and a great collection of humorous and true stories and the *Golden Circle Secrets* come alive.

Dale lives in Kennebunk, Maine.

BEN MIDGLEY

Ben Midgley has been in the fitness industry for 13 years. His approach has always been ethics, values, and relationships first, then profits, and year after year it has proven to work dramatically well.

Ben has an extensive background in sales and sales management both for internal and external sales teams. He has taught to the fitness industry all over the United States and Canada through industry conventions and consulting and is an industry leader and trendsetter. He is a previous faculty member of the International Health Racquet & Sports Club Association's Institute of Professional Club Management. Ben is a regular contributing writer for national and international fitness industry publications and was honored as the Salesperson of the Year in the $15 billion fitness industry by the International Health Racquet & Sports Club Association.

Ben is currently the senior director of corporate sales, for 24-Hour Fitness, the world's largest privately owned fitness company. He oversees the relationships of more than 3,000 corporate clients, including many of the countries best-known corporations and the business-to-business sales results of 37 corporate sales managers.

Ben has also been recognized by the California Joint Assembly as one of only 12 members appointed to the California Joint Assembly's Task Force on Youth and Workplace Wellness, developed to address the growing concern of rising health care costs in California.

Index

For additional information visit

www.goldencircle.biz